MW01268908

"A thorough exploration of one of the most pressing problems in marketing: How to cope with the complexities of the digital world. Ken Weiss surveys the situation in detail and finds hope for the future."

Al Ries co-author, *The 22 Immutable Laws of Branding* and *War in the Boardroom.*

"Today, customers experience brands on their own terms and timetables. Perceptions are shaped by their experiences in the store, on the phone or at the website. Brands must delight their customers through whatever interactive choices their customers make. *Slightware* is a user manual for the new age of electronic engagement. Read it and hope your competition doesn't."

Paul Gillin author, *The New Influencers* and *Secrets of Social Media Marketing*

Slightware

The Next Great Threat to Brands

Kenneth J. Weiss

Copyright © 2009 by Kenneth J. Weiss. All rights reserved.
Published by Hilltop Towers Publishing, Stow, Ohio.

ISBN – 10
0615279228

ISBN – 13
978-0-615-27922-0

Library of Congress Control Number
2009927611

No part of this book may be used or reproduced in any
manner without written permission except in the case of
quotations used in articles and reviews. Any person com-
mitting an unauthorized act may be liable to criminal prose-
cution and civil claims for damages. For specific exceptions
governed by a Creative Commons Attribution-
NonCommercial-ShareAlike License visit
www.Slightware.com

Special thanks to editors Barbie Weiss, Mark Morelli and
Jill Bailin.

This book may be purchased for educational, business, or
promotional use. For more information contact the author,
KennethJWeiss@gmail.com.

The origin of this book can be traced to a column I penned for *CrainTech*, a sibling publication of *Crain's Business*, in 2002. The primary reaction at the time was, admittedly, a mix of raised eyebrows and curious looks. A few years have changed everything. The Internet has evolved into Web 2.0, and every corner of the enterprise is being crammed with software.

Technology's foothold is allowing it to exert pressure in all directions. And that pressure is being applied to brands.

Is this a technology book about branding, or a branding book about technology?

Read it and let me know.

KennethJWeiss@gmail.com

About the Infographics

A few of the infographics from the book are available online at www.Slightware.com. The infographics cover some of the many facets of user experience and online branding. They are all governed by a Creative Commons copyright which allows you to use them for presentations, lectures and other non-commercial works. You can even create derivatives as long as you follow the Creative Commons guidelines.

The infographics are made with Microsoft Visio. This is a program usually reserved for dry, technical diagrams: flow-charts, wire frames, network diagrams—you've seen the like. With a little imagination, however, you can do some pretty amazing things.

Contents

Chapter Three

Chapter Four

Chapter Five

Chapter One

Slightware – Bigger and Badder Than Brochureware

When the web hit the mainstream in the 90s, companies fumbled through hype and skepticism and began to move their brands online. Versions "one point oh-well" of company websites were nothing more than dissected brochures pasted into the web.

Brochureware was born.

Luckily, companies soon realized that cut-and-paste was a very poor strategy. The web was dramatically different from every previous opportunity to build brands.

As technology continues to accelerate at a near unimaginable pace, a second new reality is emerging:

Brand building is fundamentally changing from a one-way transmission through media and marketing to a two-way transaction powered by software.

Once again, the initial step of brands into this new era of technology will not go well. Brand and software will not be entwined gracefully. Done poorly, digital experiences will be slightly "off brand." Done very badly, the brand will be slighted. This is the age of *Slightware*.

1

Brand purists will say that there have always been non-media related brand building activities. Companies have artfully plied the crafts of packaging, customer service, event marketing, sales promotion and others.

But now, it's different. Now, consumers can approach brands rather than waiting for brands to approach them. Customers are informed. They are empowered by the ability to set prices, configure products and un-bundle the value-adds that companies have been piling on. They also have a greater voice in the marketplace. And they can demand customized experiences. These interactions, these transactions, are being powered by software.

So what is Slightware?

Slightware is a poorly branded software-powered experience that directly or indirectly touches customers. Slightware can include customer self-service applications like those used to power call centers and web applications. It can also be "near-customer" software such as the software that companies use to guide their relationship with the customer and control marketing programs. Slightware can also be found deeper within companies. Software that is used to manage knowledge and make decisions may also exist in a bland, unbranded, form.

Slightware is festering in every corner of the economy. Here are a few common examples where slightware is a powerful and damaging force in the customer experience.

A small Midwestern truck dealership has built a reputation for fair prices and great service through two generations of hard work. It carries the best lines, and the service department is known for its ability to get drivers on the road. Late one

2

Wednesday afternoon a driver pulls in – something under the hood is just not right. The driver takes a seat in a comfortable lounge surrounded by manufacturer posters for the latest model of the truck he drives. He picks up a brochure and admires the sleek shots of the truck on the open road. His rig is old and getting older. Maybe its time to take that leap. He tosses the brochure aside and begins to thumb through the most recent trade magazine. There's that truck again. "Just maybe," he thinks.

Back in the shop the mechanic is getting to work. It's late, but this is his first chance to work on a model this old. One look under the hood, and he knows he's in trouble. He heads to the phone to call technical support for the truck's manufacturer. He knows that "Pete" has been at the company forever and has lived through almost every model change. Several voice prompts later an unfamiliar voice is on the phone. Pete no longer works there, but the new person would be happy to help. The mechanic gives the agent some basic information about the truck, and his assessment of what might be wrong. The tech support person is confused. He types some basic queries into the new technical support database, but none of the answers are applicable. He tries to access the service manual in the digital library, but it does not go back far enough. The "support person" says that he will need to transfer the call. A few clicks later, and the mechanic is left with the sound of a dial tone. The mechanic calls back. Eventually, another new voice, who incidentally answers the phone in a different manner, repeats the same steps, and still has no answers. In one burst of inspiration he types a search into the brand's website. He gives the mechanic the name and number of a dealer who might be able to help. "That's us," the mechanic snarls back.

The mechanic heads to the waiting room, and gives the driver the news: The manufacturer does not have an answer for the problem. The mechanic relays the story about the phone and voices, but he has an idea. The dealership's weekend mechanic might have an answer. Twenty minutes later the weekend guy

3

pulls in and introduces himself to the driver. After a brief series of questions he heads to the garage. An hour later the truck is idling smoothly in front of the building. As the driver heads out the waiting room, he decides that it is time to get a new rig, and this is the place to get it; but as he catches one last glance of the poster, he is sure that it won't be that one, from that company. In the back, the mechanic wipes down his tools and makes a mental note to chat with the sales people tomorrow.

Now, what chance do more ads, brochures and posters have to create any positive brand effect with either the driver or the mechanic?

What happens when the software is a little closer to the consumer? Perhaps beginning with a website.

It is Christmas any time in the last few years. Dad, the present hunter, heads to his closest big box retailer. Mission: Buy a large children's playhouse. He knows the brand. He knows the model. He has seen it on the retailer's website. This should be easy. Dad strolls the aisles, looks in the obvious spots, and being a thoroughly modern guy, decides to ask for help. The clerk looks puzzled. He's never seen that playhouse. The manager soon arrives with the explanation. They don't like to stock those at the store because they need too much shelf space. Dad knows what the manager is going to say before it is said. "You can get it at the website." Later that night, Dad logs on, sifts through the browser history and is soon staring at the playhouse. One simple line warms his heart: "In stock - usually ships in 3-5 days." Plenty of time. Perfect. One click and it is in the cart. The site asks him if he would like to pick it up at his nearest store. That would be convenient, and that option does not have a shipping charge. He completes the order and reads through the instructions for checking order status. Dad logs off happy.

Two days later the website shows that his order has shipped. A few days after that Dad stops by the store. Confusion reigns.

4

The people at the customer service desk stare at his email receipt like it is in cuneiform. (That's a cryptic ancient form of writing for the non-history buffs.) The manager appears and once again says that they do not carry those. Shelf space and all that. The manager says that the website help is his best shot at an answer.

The next day Dad checks the site to see the message: "Delivered." Deciding to save the drive, Dad calls the store. Yes, the truck delivered, but once again - no playhouse. Dad finally calls the 800 number. The rep confides that the store uses an outside logistics company, and their systems are not tied to the website. The programming logic in the site simply estimates the delivery based upon the item leaving inventory. The playhouse, unfortunately, is also an item that the stores will not receive because of shelf space issues. Neither the rep nor the website is sure where the playhouse is being held.

The website, which served its purpose perfectly in the beginning, turned out to be a poor brand experience.

Slightware Can Get Big

For some organizations slightware is not a matter of a rogue software application being installed on one or two computers, or a handful of people doing bad PowerPoint presentations. In many instances the line between brand and slightware is a haze that envelops the entire enterprise.

The leadership of a large university speaks optimistically about the role of the web in delivering the university's vision and extending its mission. Almost every department, program and professor has an idea. The ability to create and to publish through web systems has been construed as the right of autonomous brand representation. Unfortunately, no one spends any time understanding the brand dynamics of the organization's loosely connected websites, content repositories, web-based applications, intranets and extranets.

The sheer volume of slightware emanating from the university is staggering.

- Course catalogs are launched as searchable documents, but class registration is handled by a different system. Students have to copy information from the catalogs and manually enter the data in order to register.

- Many departments and colleges have their own sites. Others only exist online as a collection of PDF files.

- Some professors post class materials in a central university provided location, while others post syllabi on their personal sites.

- Students use separate systems to retrieve email, check grades and submit assignments.

- The athletic department, alumni relations staff and development office each try to reach alumni and parents via different websites.

- Orbiting this quagmire is a universe of websites for technology transfer initiatives, publications, advocacy groups, clubs, Greek organizations and more.

This amalgam of systems has numerous problems, apart from the obvious:

- There is little, if any, integration of the navigation.

- The style and visual devices used throughout all of the interfaces are vastly different.

- The university logo is used incorrectly in various places.

- Referential content leads to multiple pop-ups.

6

- Best practices for browser and monitor resolution compliance are not consistently enforced.

The disconnected nature of the web systems has an immeasurable negative impact on the user experience:

- Any user who becomes familiar with one site or system does not have a head start in any of the university's other sites. Each must be learned independently, and the user is forced to sort through the inconsistencies.

- Search engines present users with an upside-down version of the university. Obscure content published as static pages ranks high while the strategically and artfully created pages coming from content management systems are buried deep within the search results.

- A user attempting to navigate the university web presence cannot sense the boundaries of the system. Sometimes they keep looking for content by following links. Other times they give up too early because the site map or navigation does not indicate the presence of other sites.

- Rarely are the search functions of the sites working in harmony. The results found using one site differ dramatically from the results generated from another.

The university slightware problem is getting worse. Speed-to-publish, the demand for innovation, the evolution of technologies and improved content creation skills will put an even greater strain on the university brand.

Oh, yeah—the university has its regular .edu website, too.

Slightware is Everywhere

Slightware is present in email, on the phone, in text messages, on the fax machine, in corporate presentations, behind the counter at stores and in front of the merchandise as a kiosk. You'll find it in schools, homes, offices, warehouses, public spaces and everywhere in between in the mobile world. You'll also find lots of it in the world of Web 2.0.

The only thing more frightening than the potential magnitude and frequency of slightware is how remarkably ordinary it has come to seem:

An accounting firm takes a long weekend and fails to change the message on its automated phone system.

The human resources software package used by a company truncates job titles on the website. The southwest administrative assistant becomes a "southwest administrative ass."

The underside of 30,000 contest bottlecaps are accidentally inscribed with "system error" when the application driving the laser printer fails to handle the contest logic.

A search engine unable to distinguish between different users at the same household presents a strange assortment of "targeted" ads based upon the accumulated searches and viewed pages. Mom and Dad are perplexed, and more than a little upset, about the ads Junior is seeing.

Hackers create an automated script that repeatedly plays a game on a new product's website. Unfortunately the hackers insist on collecting the prize based upon a loophole in the rules. Nobody gets anything except the brand, which gets a black eye.

An email circulates around the internet showing a picture of a ruthless dictator drinking a well-known beverage brand. Of course it wasn't a real picture, but just an image that someone created with simple photo editing software.

Kenneth J. Weiss

Using a free email account and fake user name, a disgruntled employee systematically posts damaging financial information about his previous employer on a web message board.

A small company hires a college student to help them get their website listed in search engines. The student creates hundreds of phantom pages laced with their competitors' brand names. He thinks this is a good idea. Unfortunately he does not know that this tactic is frowned upon by search engines, and may get the site blackballed.

Several ministers pool their resources and hire a local firm to email an inspirational thought for the day to several thousand congregants. The firm mixes up its lists and the churchgoers receive an obscene joke instead of an uplifting message.

A person calls the cable company to dispute a charge on a current monthly bill, only to be trapped in an endless warren of phone prompts.

The graphic design intern for a chemical company retrieves an image from an asset database and emails the file to a sales rep. The distributor loves the presentation, especially the 16oz. bottle of radiator fluid. Unfortunately that product had been discontinued. That information was not associated with the image, and the intern had no way of knowing.

During the first week of each month, a widow goes to her mailbox and finds a magazine that continues to show her deceased husband's name on the mailing label. No matter how many times she leaves messages, the label does not get changed. Each month she curses them, and tells everyone she knows.

A family-focused website powered by user submissions and rankings is manipulated by a stream of fraudulent activity in order to promote a college savings program to parents.

9

The GPS system on a rental car conveniently records "recent places." The next person who rents the car immediately loses their interest in touching the steering wheel.

A wiki listing is deceitfully hijacked by people wanting to smear a political candidate.

A company signs up for a $99 online web promotion package. They enter some data and pay with a credit card. Later they find out that their site was listed on hundreds of spam web pages with other unrelated sites for gambling and pornography.

Customers attempting to download a free white paper from a consulting firm encounter an onerous registration form.

A company builds a website that is virtually unusable unless the user has a broadband connection and an obscure plug-in.

A restaurant manager finds the bus boy and a waitress, who happens to be his daughter, exchanging recipes in the break room. The bus boy is fired. On his way out, the ex-employee changes the message on the outdoor animated sign. Everyone on Highway 6 learns something new about the waitress. The manager, unable to run the software, has to pull the plug on the sign during the busiest night of the week.

Where did each become slightware?

Getting It Right

Before you reach for your Rapidographs, line tape, ad slicks and radio donut scripts (all ancient branding tools), know that there is hope. Technology, the accelerant that feeds the slightware conflagration, is rocket fuel in disguise.

Look what happens when technology is successfully infused with the brand.

The mother of an infant sees a TV spot for the local grocer out of the corner of her eye. The dewy produce glistens. The baker smiles. The aisles are wide and clean. Later that week the mother heads to the store. Out from among the cacophony of labels, signage and POP, her shopping cart emerges. She goes to check out, presents her loyalty card and the purchases are tallied. Her receipt spews from the register, and she expectantly flips it over. Diaper coupons! Yes, diaper coupons. Each carrying the logo of the manufacturer – and the grocer.

Which was the more powerful brand experience? The TV spot? The labels? The signage? The POP? Or the diaper coupons created on the fly just for her? Find a mother. Ask her. (If you haven't caught on yet, it's the diaper coupons.)

Here's another:

Two different couples are considering a cruise; both have been on a cruise before and had a great experience. Coincidently, their first cruises were at the exact same time on the exact same ship, and both couples wistfully stare at calendars marked with the same date. They will unknowingly travel together again.

As they are making their plans, each couple receives a brochure from the cruise line. Serendipity is playfully at work again because the brochures came off the press next to each other. The pictures are precisely everything each couple remembers. The schedule, printed inside the back cover, is full of the activities that they are sure to enjoy. The cruise will feature some of the same entertainers they saw previously along with a few new ones. The brochure even notes some of the special meals that they adored their first time.

Make sense so far? Sure.

Well, one couple is in their seventies, likes guided tours of historic sites, enjoys big band music and prefers American cuisine.

11

The second couple is in their twenties, lives to scuba dive, prefers Latino pop music and only eats vegan.

Did these couples get the same brochure? Of course not. The brochures were printed by a digital print system tied to a content management application governed by a rules database of previous customer history and planned ship activities. Even though the brochures came off the press consecutively, they are completely different. The images, colors, copy and schedules were dynamically generated and committed to paper to stir the particular enthusiasms of each specific couple.

These couples will again be on the same ship at the same time, but will each have the completely different and unique experience shown in their brochure.

These different couples with different tastes had the same great exposure to the same brand because of technology.

Here's a case where the sound orchestration of strategy and technology is used to manage a brand's relationship with myriad constituents:

Tucked beside a river in a small southern city is a hospital. Healthcare choices in the area are few. Well, one, actually. Does it have a monopoly? Probably. But the administration of the hospital is dedicated to maintaining the institution's reputation within the community.

Take a look at what the brand means to the people who live in the area:

- A group of siblings deeply moved by the care their mother received in the last days of her life makes a donation in memoriam.

12

- Two parents elated with the outcome of their child's surgical procedure arrange a southern barbeque for the operating team.

- Over 500 people sign up for a cancer walk to benefit the oncology department. Each person enlists the backing of several sponsors.

- After hitting it big, the founder of a software company makes a substantial gift to the hospital.

- Throughout the year, dinners, auctions, art shows and rummage sales are held to benefit the hospital. The events are organized and operated by an army of volunteers.

In each instance, the individuals – call them consumers if you like – have gone beyond the bounds of mere brand loyalty. How does the hospital maintain this momentum of good will? By providing outstanding care, obviously. But also critical to the success of the brand is the skillful management of communications and relationships. One element of that effort is a centralized fundraising and event-planning software application.

- Every monetary gift is immediately followed by a personalized letter of thanks which also serves as a tax receipt.

- Individuals in the community only receive solicitation mailings if they fit a very carefully constructed profile, and suggested contribution amounts are driven by data about the recipient.

- Attendees at events receive carefully personalized invitations, reminders, nametags, programs and, of course, thank you notes.

- Save-the-date postcards are sent to individuals based upon a relationship mapping software module that targets groups of people who attended previous events together.

- Fifteen monthly department newsletters are created and mailed to different lists. Some people receive only one while others regularly enjoy multiple editions. No person ever misses a newsletter, and no one receives a newsletter they don't want.

- Gentle reminders are automatically created with the person's name and scheduled amount for year-long pledges.

People are clearly touched by the brand, and the brand always touches them thoughtfully.

Good Can Be Small

Good branding through technology is out there. While it may not be as prevalent as slightware, inspirational examples can be found.

A father-and-son dental practice reduces the number of forgotten appointments by 80% using a computer-based phone system that automatically calls patients and reminds them with recorded messages pulled from a simple library of greetings, times and dates.

Who says the product actually needs to exist? A small manufacturing company wins a large contract by creating a DVD movie of a proposed production line that exists only in their engineering software application. The images were exported and spliced together with a simple movie editing program.

The web rocks! An unknown band, unable to get a record deal, releases its first album on the web using free tools from a social networking site. Thirteen tracks – no charge. A huge fan base

14

develops. The demand for the second album is huge. Several record companies compete for the rights. The band is huge.

A real estate agent uses a simple database to keep track of attendees at her open houses and sends them information about other listings based upon their comments. She quickly develops a reputation as an agent who listens and provides great personalized service.

Sales triple when a regional sports magazine customizes its cover using direct-to-print technology to feature the local high school teams in each of its distribution zones.

A family books an entire week at a small independently owned resort based upon the 360-degree views on the website.

A risk management consultant creates a series of blogs, each focusing on a specific vertical market. He tends to them rigorously. Within six months he is selectively answering RFPs. He only submits responses for projects that fit his long-term vision: Work that helps get better work, and work that lets him spend more time at home.

Using carefully selected tags and phrases a young photographer posts her college portfolio on a public photo sharing website. In less than a year she is operating her own small studio specializing in shots featuring children.

A catalog website uses a multivariate program to test numerous marketing offers. Customers buy more. They are happy. The catalog? Yes, happy too.

The marketing manger of small heating contractor uses data from the town's building department, a mailing list, a color printer and a simple mail merge program to create custom letters. The detailed messages and introductory offer make him look informed and credible.

15

Customers are given the ability to watch the progress on the construction of their office space when a large general contractor feeds webcam images to a password-protected website.

A small, frozen food delivery business combines its order system, inventory program, telephone system and route management software to notify customers by phone of delivery times. Customers spend less time waiting at home. The trucks are on the road for fewer miles.

Unable to consistently generate repeat website traffic, a raw material supplier distributes a desktop application that automatically displays updated prices on a variety of bulk chemicals. A sizable number of purchases are made, but the real value comes from the increased brand awareness as hundreds of companies put the application on their desktops.

A regional sales manager helps the staff double the number of appointments by combining trade show attendee data with an email template that includes links to video case studies.

Chat and an online video fashion show become the focal point of a cosmetic company's effort to create awareness and demand for a new line of ethnicity-specific products. It works. Hundreds of questions and answers are associated to clips from the show. Retailers are deluged with requests for the products.

An enterprise software company attempting to crack a large account uses a content management system to create small websites, referred to as microsites, with information tailored to each senior executive.

A crash scene simulation company garners over 1,400 hours of lawyers' time (which was probably billed anyway) by engaging the lawyers in a branded online game.

So, What Happens Now?

Slightware is everywhere. It powers the systems that customers use to interact with companies. It powers the systems that employees use to assist customers. It powers the tools that employees use to create, publish and disseminate information.

And it is more. It is the systems that enable people to publish their own editorial content. It is the systems that allow 3rd parties to represent products and brands.

When businesses began to move their brands online in the '90s the first step was placing information online. Brochures were cut-and-pasted to the web. It didn't work, and companies soon knew brochureware was not the answer.

Now, digital systems are becoming more pervasive, and a parallel epiphany lies in the not-too-distant future:

Data, functionality, rules and models will not be enough to create, present, grow and preserve brands. Systems will need to be infused with the brand at their elemental level. Otherwise, they will simply exist as Slightware.

Offline advertising, public relations and other marketing activities will always play a role in the creation of brand awareness, but the true job of brand building will be done through software and systems.

17

What You Will Find in This Book

This work represents the meeting point of the power of brands and the inevitability of software—not a middle ground where each side offers concessions, but rather, it is the definition of a new space. It will show you what to avoid and what to envision.

Chapter 1
Slightware - Bigger and Badder than Brochureware
You've just read it.

Chapter 2
Brand Jive: Nuts, Bolts and Economic Alchemy
Every thing you need to understand brands: terminology, construction, measurement, and an explanation of how brands create value.

Chapter 3
Understanding User Experience, or "UX is the Crux of Slightware"
A detailed explanation of User Experience including the types of user experiences, the dynamics of content in digital experiences and a simple distillation of the fundamentals of user experience.

Chapter 4
The Causes of Slightware
See what you are fighting against. This chapter covers Slightware forces within organizations and the vast network of forces outside of companies. Many of the infographics not available online are contained within this chapter.

Chapter 5
Beating Slightware – How To, Why To and Who To
Here are just a few of the great topics in this chapter: under-standing usability, beating the creeps, identifying skill sets, examining users experiences and finishing touches. (You may just be tempted to skip to this section. But don't.)

Don't Forget www.Slightware.com

When you visit <u>www.Slightware.com</u> you'll find a selection of infographics covering a variety of topics in the book. Not only are they available in pdf format, but you will also find the source files so you can create your own derivatives. As the reader community creates new versions, they too will be available at <u>www.Slightware.com.</u>

20

Kenneth J. Weiss

Chapter Two

Brand Jive:
Nuts, Bolts and Economic Alchemy

A thousand answers have been offered for the question, "What is a brand?"

The best is the simplest.

A Brand Is "Meaning with Economic Value"

Brands can be products, services, people, events, experiences and even ideas. Brands can encompass every aspect of a company and can be defined by incredibly small elements. But in the end, brands create meaning, and companies develop brands to create value.

The standard B-school definition sounds something like this: "Brands are far more than logos wrapped in corporate identity packages, and brands can be found in many more places than the store shelf. A brand is the complete bundle of tangible and intangible assets associated with a product, service or company." This is a great start for understanding brands. A brand can be defined through some combination of a visual language, a specific approach to product development, the tenor of the messages which surround it, the behavior of the company that owns it, the leverage the brand creates in the marketplace, and the long-term value it creates on the corporate balance sheet.

Good brands create meaning in the mind of the consumers, and create a shortcut to the answers for questions around trust, quality, performance and credibility. Good brands work in conjunction with pricing strategies and distribution strategies to ultimately shape the bottom line.

The Brand Vector Model

Most brand models share a shockingly similar number of characteristics. This may be coincidence, or just like science's periodic table, it may be that brand researchers have independently distilled brands to the same common elements.

The Brand Vector model, too, shares some characteristics with other models, but is ultimately governed by a simple principle: A brand cannot mean all things to all people. A brand inherently has direction, its own vector. Within the vector are forces. When the forces are aligned, the brand maintains its course and momentum. When things get ragged, a wobble ensues, and a brand can eventually "lose its way."

How is the Brand Vector model unique? This model, unlike other models, goes both deeper into the company as a point of origination and further into the market. It starts with all facets of a company and recognizes that the market is not just a recipient of the brand, but a participant in the process. More importantly, the Brand Vector model addresses the reality of technology's role in the brand.

Kenneth J. Weiss

by Kenneth J. Weiss

The Brand Vector Model

The Brand Vector

The Brand Countenance

Campaigns
Signature Cues
Customer Experiences
Branded Environments
The Market Echo

The Brand Composition

Position
Name System
Visual Identity System
Brand Posture
Reason To Believe
Associations

The Brand Construct

Soul
Personality
Brand Attributes
Promise
Voice

The Brand Culture

Leadership
People Passion
Financial Climate
Physical Environment
Knowledge Systems
Market Approach
Operations
Brand Accumen

Flexible

External

Fixed

Internal

This infographic is governed by the Creative Commons
Attribution-Non-Commercial ShareAlike 2.5 License.
creativecommons.org

(cc) SOME RIGHTS RESERVED

www.Slightware.com

The Brand Vector has four forces:

The Brand Culture: The environment that owns and is ultimately responsible for the brand.

The Brand Construct: The fundamental definition and mission of the brand.

The Brand Composition: The more tangible and perceptible elements that communicate the brand.

The Brand Countenance: The expression and composure of the brand across all activities.

The vector behaves differently as you move away from its origination, the Brand Culture, to its existence in the marketplace, the Brand Countenance. The first continuum is fixed-to-flexible. Elements of the Brand Culture are fixed. At most they evolve gradually over time. The Brand Countenance changes more rapidly in the form of new advertising campaigns, redesigned packaging or new store layouts. The second continuum is internal-to-external. The elements of the Brand Culture are expressed within the walls of the organization and are used as guidance. As the vector moves away from the organization, the elements become expressed outwardly to the market.

The Brand Culture

Can any company have a great brand? Can any company have a great brand in any market? Can any company have a great brand in any market at any time?

No.

24

No.

No.

These are tough answers to accept. Traditional thinking states that any problem can be tackled with enough resources. Having enough resources should turn any "no" into a "yes." Yes? No. Why not? Successful brands with staying power are the product of a great brand culture. Not every company has it, nor can they make it.

Leadership

The highest levels of the organization need to understand the power of branding and be respectful of the necessary steps needed to build great brands. Senior executives with sales, finance and other backgrounds need the assistance of great brand thinkers. They also need the ability to separate solid, strategic vision from personal agendas and the recommendations of consulting firms looking for new accounts and engagements.

Great brands also require continuity. Markets and audiences cannot be retrained to view a brand differently every few years or every few quarters. The purposeful, deliberate path required by brands needs to be uninterrupted by the "new thinking" of the "new guy." Not an easy thing with the average tenure of CEOs dropping like a stone.

Technology is also part of the leadership story. The CIO/CTO (Chief Information Officer or Chief Technology Officer) needs to be in the loop with the CEO (Chief Executive Officer) and CMO (Chief Marketing Officer) on all decisions, including brand decisions.

People Passion

Employees who are committed to a product or cause will always be better for the brand. Yes, there is the threat of myopia, but it is far less than the threat of indifference. Contrast the diehard naturalist who starts an organic food company to the small consumer products company that looks at the organic food niche as a market opportunity. Either one might be more successful from a sales standpoint in the long run, but who will stay fundamentally committed to the brand through every business decision? Who will be able to better understand the nuances of the product, packaging, customer service and the needs of the market? Having passionate employees is not a guarantee of brand success, but it can be a valuable contributing factor.

Financial Climate

Great brands require an investment, and they require corporate-wide sensitivity to the hundreds of decisions where brand strategy and finances mingle. If the packaging of an environmentally friendly product could be made with slightly more expensive recycled paper or cheaper new stock, which should be used? How about traditional ink versus soy-based ink? If a company is having trouble hitting sales targets for a quarter, should price points be dropped in order to move more product? How does the price contribute to the brand's desired position in the market? Brand decisions do not always "cost" companies. To the contrary, great brands can be incredible profit centers. The little daily decisions are key.

Kenneth J. Weiss

Physical Environment

Location, aesthetics, ergonomics, and the quality of basic systems and supplies contribute to the physical environment, and great physical environments are essential for morale, collaboration, recruiting and retention. Can really great concepts pour from gray fabric cubicles? Maybe. Can dramatic ideas flow from loft-like spaces where entire walls serve as community whiteboards? More likely. The character of a company's physical space at some level bleeds through to the brand.

Knowledge Systems

Knowledge and asset systems include: the ways in which all constituencies are trained about the brand, the systems that store assets (images, data and text) the processes that are used to coordinate marketing activities, and other systems that influence customer interactions. The inadequacies of the systems can be accentuated by fault lines running throughout organizations: marketing may be out of sync with sales, customer service may use different wording than investor relations, channel members may be representing the product in a different manner than the company, and so on. Strong systems are essential for keeping the organization on the same brand page and smoothing the fissures.

Market Approach

Companies that continually develop new products and enter new categories have to be great at branding. It's a table stake. Companies that push existing product lines should use the brand as part of their arsenal to defend margins and parry newcomers. Companies attempting to win back market share ideally maintain price points while building the brand. Discounters, me-toos, knock-offs, fast-buck and

27

other businesses traditionally do not have strengths in brand building. The problems arise when a company tries to be something that it has never been, and believes that just "thinking differently" or "taking a new approach" will change its branding abilities.

Operations

Operational thinking spans the entire organization. How does an order look when it is shipped? How is the main phone line answered? What is the policy for paying suppliers? Do employees enjoy their jobs? Every aspect of operations contributes to the company ecosystem in which brands live. Excellent companies can have excellent brands. Excellent brands have less tenable positions in weak companies.

Brand Acumen

Each and every employee within an organization should have an understanding of branding and an appreciation for each of the company's brands. This goes beyond abiding by corporate brand standards documentation to the ability to live the brand. Many companies have early success because the brand is in every part of the day-to-day activities for every employee. Unfortunately, that special pervasiveness deteriorates with new employees, success and other forms of change.

The Brand Construct

Every great brand is built on a set of permanent, lasting truths called the Brand Construct. The word "permanent" can be tricky. Brands by nature cannot be radically altered on a daily, weekly, monthly or even yearly basis. Do they evolve? Certainly. But simply cracking open the Pandora's box of "Let's make some changes to the direction of the brand" can be misinterpreted as an endorsement of the idea that the Brand Construct *can* or *should* be changed.

While the elements of the Brand Construct may never be outwardly expressed to the market, they guide all elements of the Brand Composition and the Brand Countenance.

Soul

The soul of the brand is a singular defining concept typically comprised of a word or a very short phrase.

The archetypical examples have always been:

Maytag = Dependability

Volvo = Safety

If a brand requires a longer, more elaborate definition it is probably not as finely focused as it should be, or the owner is attempting to keep the brand open-ended in hopes of being able to adapt to market changes.

The soul is not a mission statement, tag line or catchphrase. It is a concept against which every product, service and brand decision can be judged.

Personality

Personification is a great way to define and understand brands. Even within the most homogenous high school clique, college sorority, suburban country club or old boy's boardroom, people are vastly different. The members can feel differentiated after only a brief period of observation.

29

Guy 1: "He was the tall, but some what stooped, older gentleman who seemed to be very brusque with the support staff."

Guy 2: "He was older as well, and shared the same gray hair cut, and although reserved, seemed open to conversation when asked a question."

These differences mean a lot!

Brands can be defined the same way—through the use of terms and phrases that would be applied to people.

Here are a few brands in the high-end automobile market. Think of them as people, and guess the brand.

Guy (Brand) #1: "Very British but definitely outdoorsy. Had a certain upper-crust feeling about him, but also seemed like a person who would enjoy traveling to very remote places."

Guy (Brand) #2: "A very stylish German fellow. Well put together with a somewhat exclusive feel about him."

Guy (Brand) #3: "An older American gentleman. Likes to dress well and wear expensive watches. Has much more verve than I remembered."

Did you guess Land Rover, BMW and Cadillac?

This type of analysis, people watching, is fun and can be downright addictive. Two different people can observe another person or brand and sometimes immediately agree, or can exchange puzzled "I did not get that at all" looks. A brand, however, pointed at two members of its target audience should always elicit agreement.

30

Companies use this idea of personification to begin to make the brand tangible and understandable.

Brand Attributes

Brand attributes are words and phrases used to describe and define brands in a way that would not apply to people. For instance, a person would not be "global" in the same way that a brand would be. A person would not be described as community-based, but an organization could be.

The collection of attributes for a brand helps it find its way in a marketplace. "Locally focused" means very different things to a brand than "national." So too, does "diverse" versus "focused." The same for "proven" versus "innovative." The imaginative and purposeful melding of attributes and personality make brands as interesting as characters in some of the world's greatest literary works.

Promise

The brand's promise is the distillation of why it exists for users or consumers. What does it do? Why be interested? What's in it for me? The brand and its inherent promise won't be for everyone, but it needs to hold a promise for its intended market.

The promise needs to be ingrained throughout the entire organization. Imagine a hospital with the promise of unmatched care: The hospital has great doctors, a very fine physical environment, an approachable demeanor, and a strong local focus. Sounds good so far. What happens if the billing department chronically gets patient accounts confused? A bill is sent to the insurance company multiple times. Patients are charged directly for items that the insur-

31

ance company would typically cover. Even billing information is sometimes transposed to a different account. How does the brand promise of unmatched care feel then?

Every organization needs to be capable of delivering the brand promise. Sometimes companies and brands fail because the organization simply reaches too far. Other times the company and brands are square pegs in round holes. Still there are times the brand promise is valid, and the organization can deliver, but the market cannot generate the type of revenue needed to keep the brand going.

Voice

Brand voice includes both the delivery of the message and its tonality. Some organizations for instance attach the voice of the company to its founder or key leader for a long period of time. In that case, a person has been designated as a key element in the delivery, and the choice of words conveys the tonality. The person may speak on a television commercial, appear by way of a signature on print communications, be quoted often by reporters, and even have their picture appear. Virgin Airlines is a great brand, and Richard Branson is a key part of the voice. Google has Brin. Yahoo has Yang. This dynamic is not to be confused with a campaign that uses a spokesperson since campaigns are changed more frequently. In rare occasions a campaign element such as the Maytag repairman transitions from being a campaign element to the true voice of the brand. Some true brand geeks will argue that Charmin toilet paper lost its way when Mr. Whipple was phased out, while Perdue has gracefully passed the role of the brand voice along.

The second part of the voice is tonality. Good tonality is careful and subtle. Unfortunately it is more common to see a brand making dramatically egregious errors rather than doing it right. Some brands try to regain relevancy by becoming "hip." The tonality is laced with catch-phrases and words du jour. The brand ends up looking silly. Tonality needs to be carefully guided with smart, appropriate words, phrases, and delivery in every type of communication and experience.

The Brand Composition

As a brand vision begins to solidify, the brand takes shape through elements that will serve as the building blocks of ultimate expression in the marketplace.

Position

Articulating the brand position is a key step in determining how the brand fits into the marketplace relative to competitive brands and the needs of the target audience. Determining the brand position helps guide decisions. Can super-premium ingredients be used, or should lower-priced versions be used to help hit the price point? Will the margins on this project support heavy advertising, or will channel partners be required to do more of the sales and marketing? In some instances, the brand's position is deliberately attached to a competitor's. Knock-off brands attempt to be dead ringers. Sometimes two brands under the same company are used in tandem to capture two distinct segments of the market. In other instances companies attempt to find clear space for the brand.

Once the position is determined, it needs to be communicated and established in the mind of the market. Like other elements at this point of the brand vector, it can evolve, but not radically shifted in a short period of time.

Name System

Creating or selecting the name of a brand is not easy. Any possible name is subject to strategic, cultural and technical considerations. Brand names also are governed by tricky copyright and trademark laws. Nothing is worse for a marketing department than investing heavily in a product launch, only to be sued by a competitor for trademark infringement.

The market may have a part in steering the brand name. Imagine a law firm with an oddly techie-sounding name in a sea of Bigshot, Bigshot & Bigshot names. The techno name might be logical if the firm specialized in technology issues, but would make little sense if the lawyers focused on family law or real estate.

Cultural issues, both "pop" and "multi," have been historically tough on brands. Brands can be torpedoed by a one-hit-wonder music act that shares the same name. Brands can be tainted by an unintentional endorsement from an objectionable character. Word roots and letter combinations do not always mean the same things in foreign countries as they do in their country of origin. The possible pitfalls of cultural issues are almost endless.

Technology considerations during the naming process have come to the forefront in the dot com era. The simplest test: Can the brand name be secured as www.brandname.com? If not, who has it? What is similar? If there is a common typo, where does it go? Should the name be secured in other countries such as www.brandname.jp? Can the name be easily entered on mobile devices by thumbing? Is there a natural truncation that should be secured as well?

The name often exists as part of a more complicated naming system. For instance, a food might come in two slightly different flavors such as XYZ Barbeque Sauce and XYZ Barbeque Sauce with Southern Smoke. Some brand names are built with this in mind. Others get that NASCAR fender-feel after being layered with additional words and characters. Brand names might also exist as an ingredient to other brands such as ABC Computers with INTEL or 123 Lawn tractors with Briggs and Stratton engines.

Naming strategies tend to change over time. Fifty years ago the world was full of names like "Atlas," "Pinnacle" and other exemplary sounding words derived from Greek and Latin terms. At one time "empty vessel" names were in vogue. These were words (sometimes just odd combinations of letters) that had no inherent meaning. They were "empty" and needed to be filled through brand building efforts. The dot com era brought a new level of weirdness. Strange combinations of words were juxtaposed, correct spelling was passé, capitalization was open to interpretation, and "webby" names were ginned together with lots of x, y and z's mixed in. Some stuck and became commonplace: eBay, YouTube, Flickr, etc. Others faded into the dotcom dead pool.

Visual Identity System

The visual identity system of a brand is made up of its logo, colors, fonts, symbols and other visual elements. Nike for instance has the logotype of the word Nike and the logo-gram of the Swish. Tiger Woods, a Nike pitchman, has made wearing a red shirt on Sundays part of the visual brand language for him and Nike. Some companies might make their corporate headquarters building or a mascot part of the visual identity system.

Companies with multiple brands have the challenge of or-chestrating a sea of visual elements. Sometimes the goal is to create visually harmonious and self-explanatory, familial relationships between the brands. Other times the goal is to create distinct differentiation. Sometimes the goal is to do a little of both.

In the past, corporate identity systems were centered on business cards, letterhead and envelopes. These will always be important, but web sites, PowerPoint presentations, and even the graphics in email signatures get more market face time than traditional printed elements. Today's technologies let more people create communications materials which are, of course, both good and bad. People can create specifically targeted messages, but DIY design software leads to bad alterations, adaptations and bastardizations of the complete identity system.

Studying a visual identity system is a great way to see how this part of the brand vector, the Brand Composition, changes slowly over time. Changes are typically evolution-ary rather than revolutionary. Even a brand that wants to communicate a radical new direction or attitude often keeps a strong visual connection to its past.

36

Brand Posture

The brand posture is the attitude that shapes how the brand will act and react in real-life situations. For instance, if a customer's online order was delayed in shipping, what action is considered acceptable to the brand? Send the order when it is ready with no explanation? Send a "one size fits all" email? Send a form letter populated with some pertinent data? Send a personalized email from a more senior executive with a detailed explanation and apology?

Reason to Believe

"Why should I believe you?" Ouch. That question smarts. Friend to friend. Boyfriend to girlfriend. Husband to wife. Child to father. Ouch, it hurts. It's the question that calls someone on the carpet. It's the same for consumers to brands. Brands make promises to consumers. Brand X will make you happier, skinnier, financially better off, more successful, healthier, smarter, better prepared, et cetera, et cetera. The consumer says "Oh yeah? Tell me how. And tell me why." Brands want people to believe, and may also say things people want to hear. Consumers, as skeptical creatures, wipe away the sheen of the fancy copy to see if the brand can deliver.

The reason to believe goes beyond the spiel to the brand's origin. Can a brand known for producing unreliable automobiles suddenly tell the market, "Here's our line of premium-priced luxury autos!"? Can a company known for human rights violations in overseas factories launch a line of eco-friendly products because, "We care about the environment."? A brand must be capable of delivering on the promise, and the brand must have a track record that allows consumers to believe.

37

Organizational Associations

A definite line exists between having deeply rooted organizational associations and jumping on the bandwagon for the latest en vogue cause or group. Contrast the perception of a celebrity who shows up at a rally for some cause that coincidentally seems related to their latest movie, versus a company that has supported a local charity for the past 15 years. The celebrity's actions seem purely opportunistic while the company's actions look altruistic.

The Brand Countenance

Unlike the other layers of the brand vector, the elements of Brand Countenance are outwardly expressed and can change over time. Market dynamics, fads, seasonality and cultural trends, along with internal strategies and bottom-line performance shape the Brand Countenance.

Campaigns

Campaigns are no longer synonymous with advertising. Any directed effort around a particular objective can be labeled as a campaign. A company might want to capture more leads at a trade show. The training of personnel, booth design and sales materials become part of that campaign. If a bookstore is experiencing smaller transaction sales at the register, tactical changes in store layout, signage and in-store promotions could be rolled into a campaign. The end-to-end construction of a campaign needs to be deliberate and on-brand.

Signature Cues

A good brand countenance includes a series of signature cues. These are elements that should be owned, captured or

38

dominated in the marketplace by the brand. Taglines are a traditional example of a brand cue. The great tag lines "stick" and become inseparable from the brand. Signature cues can also include sound effects and other aural devices, such as the "gong" sound widely used by Taco Bell. Visual textures, product design commonalities and even aromas can be part of a brand's signature cues.

Customer Experiences

A unique customer experience can be a compelling part of an offering and a make-'em-take-notice element of the brand. Enterprise Rent-a-Car told customers, "We'll pick you up." Motel 6 quipped, "We'll keep the lights on." Many years ago Burger King proclaimed you should "Have it your way." In each case, the brand decided to make an experience element notable, marketable and, most importantly, explainable. Some companies create very unique experiences, but they are impossible to encapsulate in an easily explained phrase or image.

An experience strategy can extend into the digital world. Southwest Airlines created a desktop widget called "Ding" that notifies users of deals on airline tickets. Other companies have created browser tool bars that extend their brand into the web browsing interface.

Experiences are important. Product categories are ripe with parity and the costs of switching are low. Experiences provide points of differentiation that are harder to copy.

Branded Environments

Every environment is a branded environment. Some are intentionally good, others are unintentionally bad. Think of

39

two local tire stores. One is a mom-and-pop shop and the other is part of a nationally recognized chain. Now, zero in on the waiting rooms. One has comfortable chairs, clean restrooms, a television, recent (and crisp) magazines, and always-fresh doughnuts. As for the other? The coffee shop across the street enjoys a steady business of its tire customers. While both stores might have great service and prices, the physical environment helps shape the overall brand perceptions. Oh, BTW, which store had which waiting room? Could be either.

Gauging the impact of a branded environment is easy in places like hotels, spas, restaurants and amusement parks. In these places the branded environment is an important part of the X-factor. Unfortunately, the environment as a branded element should be considered an important part of every brand with a physical presence whether it is a mega-retail store or package drop box on the corner.

The Market Echo

The moment that brands opened themselves to user comments, reviews and ratings, the market's echo, either strong and clear or muffled and distorted, became part of branding. Various forms of the echo can be found on shopping sites, review sites, community sites, and on the brand site itself. Brands hope that their perceived authority and authenticity will make carefully constructed brand communication more valued than comments from the man on the street. This is not always the way it works out, however. The community offers a sense of truth that consumers value.

The reality of the echo must be contemplated and calculated throughout the life of the brand. It can be influenced but never completely controlled.

What Makes A Good Brand?

The world is full of bad brands and good brands. No doubt, lots are out there. Many simply add to the over-marketing miasma that makes up the current consumption-driven society. Others actually provide value.

When is a brand a good brand? When it is...

...Understandable

The target audience should "get" the brand. New brands with new products may take some time, but the target should be capable of eventually understanding the brand. Some brands and product concepts never catch on. "The customers just weren't ready." "It was before its time." Common phrases, common rationale. But maybe just symptoms of that fact that being understood was never in the cards.

...Memorable

Being memorable is a rare characteristic in a media-saturated world. Sure, advertising campaigns get a lot of buzz, but often consumers have a hard time connecting the brand to the campaign. Memorable brands are ones where the consumer not only knows the name, but can also describe what it offers. Being memorable requires having all forms of execution being consistently on-brand. Being interesting and creative does not hurt either.

41

...Distinct

Brands can be distinct within their categories and also distinct within the market. For instance, a brand of salad dressing may stand apart from all others in the salad dressing category and also be distinct from all other products in the realm of condiments.

Imagine a very focused (perhaps myopic) company that does all of the legwork for a new brand within their industry. The Marketing VP takes the work home to show his spouse, and the wife says, "Wow, that really feels a lot like blank." If that quick association is within the category - that's a big problem. If it is within the marketplace—that's still a problem.

...Original

Yawn....I've seen that before. Being original is tough. Brands are in competition with both their contemporary counterparts and all of the brands that have lived before. Consumers love nostalgia. They will know if a brand is attempting to "borrow" the leverage of a previous brand, or if it is truly creating something new.

...Ownable

Quick! What brand is this? "The undeniable leader in our category known for quality and innovation backed by the skill and dedication of our employees." Although that's not the best brand definition, the point is clear: many brands have created an un-original position that they can never own. In addition to originality issues, over-complexity or being defined too generically can stop a brand from ever being owned.

42

...Defensible

Business plans typically include sections that outline barriers to entry - quite literally, "what's stopping us or anybody else from getting into this space." If you are entrenched in a business, barriers to entry are a good thing. They keep your competition out. The same holds true for brands. A properly constructed brand can be defended. Individual elements or the collective whole should be able to stop competitors from jumping easily into that space.

...Relevant

Relevancy is in the mind of the target. Since brands can, and should, mean something to a specific target, understanding the target's perception is big—really big. Many brands fail because they rely on internal expertise to deliver "what customers want." Properly executed research is essential. Ideally by an external firm.

...Preemptive

What's the next big thing? What's the next small thing? What's the next technology thing? Brands need to be resolute but they cannot be blind. Culture, technology, business and values change. A good brand is envisioned with some amount of open road ahead, and should be managed in a way that prevents others from leapfrogging into that space.

...Price-Compatible

Luxury brands are doomed once they start to appear in the dollar bin. Likewise, bargain-basement brands have little chance of being the talk of the Hamptons. The brand strategy must be inline with the price and product strategy.

43

...Baggage-Free

Does the brand have any odd connotations hanging around its neck? Can a county music record label be based in Milwaukee? Can a "green" brand outsource its manufacturing to China? Can a university make a strong case to parents while telling professors that research is more important than lecturing? Hundreds of contradictions and problems like these exist, and granted, many are in the operational or execution layers, but it is not uncommon for a brand to have baggage at its most basic levels.

Measuring Brands

The business, investment and marketing communities have long realized that strong brands provide leverage. But how strong is a brand? According to whom? Measured by what? Brand hubris and true value are two very different things. The rapidly growing discipline of brand valuation brings a sound, repeatable and definable methodology to this issue.

Understanding the scope and power of a brand is a critical component in two important areas: brand management and general business management.

Brand Management

Brand Performance Management: Are brand-building efforts working? Is the brand slipping? Understanding the health of the brand lets companies monitor their progress.

Brand Portfolio Management and Budget Allocation: Understanding the upside of brands and market open space in conjunction with business modeling can help companies determine the allocation of marketing dollars.

44

Brand Architecture Planning: As brands rise and fall, the overall arrangement of brands within a company portfolio, commonly referred to as the brand architecture, can be managed to insure that all of the dominoes do not topple at the same time.

Brand Extension: Even though brand purists disdain the idea of overextending brands, brand measurement can be used to determine if a brand name can be used for a new product, placed within a new channel such as the internet or leased as part of a licensing agreement.

Business Management

Financial Reporting: Brands represent economic value. While the laws regarding the inclusion of brands in financial reports vary from country to country, it is universally accepted that good brands are worth more than bad brands.

Licensing Agreements: Companies can create additional revenue by licensing their brands. This may include allowing other companies to put a current brand name on a non-competing product, or allowing a company to use a retired brand name. The strength of the brand is a foundational part of the terms of the licensing relationship.

Joint Ventures: Companies often join forces for manufacturing, marketing and distribution projects. The strength of the brand is an important part of what a company brings to the table.

Mergers, Acquisitions and Sales: Brand strength can be an important part of M&A activity. Strong brands can be at-

45

tractive to other companies. A weak brand can even be attractive if the acquiring company feels the brand has underdeveloped potential. The strength of the brand sometimes referred to as goodwill, impacts the amount an acquiring company is willing to spend.

Dissecting Brand Value

The complete value picture of a brand is called brand equity. Dozens of models exist. Some models divide brand equity into small, weighted components where the parts and importance vary by industry, market, etc. Several of these brand equity elements, however, are found in almost every model.

Brand Awareness

In a media-saturated world, being known counts for something - it means that a brand can spend its time positioning, differentiating and explaining rather than just trying to be remembered. Brand awareness has two dimensions: unaided awareness and aided awareness. To measure unaided awareness, a series of test subjects are asked to name brands in a particular category. No tips or hints are given. When the subject cannot recall any more names, prompts are provided. This structured format determines unaided and aided brand awareness.

Brand Consideration

Knowing about a brand does not necessarily mean a person would consider buying that brand. Consumers can quickly come up with a list of cars they would never purchase, stores they would never shop, sports teams they would never watch, and so on. They know the brand, but would not consider it. The reason for the delta between awareness and consideration is an interesting point to ponder when evaluating product quality, past customer satisfaction, distribution methods and other dynamics.

Brand Loyalty

Brand loyalty measures both a consumer's proclivity to switch or not to switch, and their acceptance of changes in quality, performance or delivery.

Price Premium

Price premium is a measure of how much more the market is willing to spend for the brand without having an unfavorable effect on sales volume or market share.

Brand Quality

Brand quality is the perceived and expected performance of a product or service carrying a specific brand. A brand can be successfully managed with high or low brand quality perception measures. A brand name of canned corn found in a grocery store would be expected to have a nice color, uniform kernels and just the right amount of water. The store brand might be expected to have more irregular kernels, a little less color and a bit more water. Both might enjoy successful sales and satisfied customers if the quality delivered matches the quality that was expected.

Brand Associations

Brands can build powerful and lasting associations with people, organizations, places and cultural trends. These associations lend meaning to the brand and give consumers a shortcut to understanding the brand. A record label in New Orleans? Probably known for jazz. A university associated

47

with Carl Sagan? Probably has good science programs. An organization founded during the Great Depression? Most likely understands the plight of the poor.

Brand Advocacy

Brand advocacy is the willingness of a consumer to recommend a brand. Fred Reicheld's book *The Ultimate Question* studies this aspect of brand equity in great detail.

Brand Understanding

Brands are "known" for certain things. Sometimes these are good, other times a company wants to change perceptions or alter the mix. The depth of the understanding and the complexity of the meaning represent value. A brand that can be accurately and completely articulated by consumers is more valuable than a brand that elicits superficial and inconsistent descriptions.

Brand Metrics and Competing Brands

Each of these brand equity elements can include an analysis of competing brands often expressed as a visual map. These brand maps provide relative points to better understand the brand and to identify open areas, or whitespace, which may represent an opportunity for the brand. Not all opportunities are possibilities. Brand movements are tethered to economic, operational and market dynamics. A low awareness brand may certainly want to increase awareness but may not be able to generate the profits needed to justify an expensive advertising campaign. Another brand may want to occupy a particular space in a brand map only to discover that a competitor has a tenacious hold on that space.

48

Brand Equity Can Be A Bad Thing

Brand equity can also be negative. Call it baggage, if you will. Even if a company chooses to discontinue a brand, bad karma can linger. Edsel. Union Carbide. Vanilla Ice. New Coke. Ishtar. Most likely one of these names induces an icky feeling. So what can cause negative equity?

Perspective

Brands are designed to resonate with a target audience. Individuals outside of the target may have an immediate negative reaction. For instance, a person might look negatively upon a brand's associations. A diehard, no-holds-barred oilman probably has a different opinion of a brand associated with Greenpeace than a person who admires Energy Star rated products. A person who prides themselves on buying only the best products probably has a less than neutral opinion of a retailer's store-brand jeans. Monitoring the proximity of the negative perceptions to the target audience and shifts in the target audience perspective is essential. This uncomfortable conversation has unfortunately occurred many times:

Working Guy: "I've read the reports. That's not really what our customers think."

Boss man: "Oh yeah, based upon what?"

Working Guy: "I know the customers."

Boss man: "Apparently, you don't."

History

Time heals all wounds right? Not always. For older generations some brands are forever associated with the Depression, wars and emotional loss.

Say "Italy" to a WWII vet. Say it to a romantic young couple. Very different perceptions.

Circumstance and Wild Cards

Shifts happen. Passionately vocal supporters can turn into critics. Scientific discovery can turn a brand to poison (like a prescription medication that is found to have previously unknown side effects). A product defect can create quality perceptions that ripple across an entire portfolio of brands.

Impossible to plan for, but in some cases inevitable.

Brands – What Consumers Think

Every brand encompasses three brands: the brand as defined, the brand as delivered and the brand as perceived. Hopefully, all three are the same. Brand definition can be done using the brand vector model. Brand delivery can be evaluated by research and testing. For example, a restaurant might have a "dry run" evening for a limited number of guests; an advertising campaign can be tested with focus groups; an auto maker may present concept cars to an enthusiast group and so on. Understanding how brands are perceived - often called brand perception - requires getting inside the mind of the market.

Understanding where a brand stands is critical. A company can determine what customers truly think about the brand

50

in its current state and also identify areas where the brand can and can not go. For instance, a brand might have a perceived "low price" attribute, and consumers might say that they do not believe that the brand could deliver on a higher-priced product. A brand can also be mapped against competing and complimentary brands to find out which brand owns certain thoughts, feelings and characteristics. In the case of new brands, consumers and the market can be analyzed to identify whitespace, or at least weak space, where a brand can be positioned for success.

Brand Understanding Tools and Concepts

Dozens if not hundreds of tools and methodologies exist for understanding how consumers perceive brands. Here are just a few.

The Focus Group

The focus group is perhaps the most traditional method of understanding consumers' perceptions of brands. A group of people are selected based upon a certain demographic or psychographic composition. They are assembled in a room and a moderator initiates a conversation in a way that does not influence or bias the group. The discussion is recorded and analyzed. In a typical research project a number of focus groups are conducted to track pre and post effects of an initiative or to mitigate any data variances that could result from looking at too narrow a set of individuals.

Surveys

Surveys are a research favorite for collecting large volumes of data. Questions on a survey can be put into all types of sequences and include sophisticated skipping, branching and conditional questions. Since surveys can cost-effectively gather a large amount of data, very detailed analysis can be conducted against small slices of the respondents while still being statistically valid. A typical example would be "Of the people who met conditions A, B and F, and who answered yes to question 5 but no to question 6, 75% selected D as the answer to question 14." This type of analysis can uncover amazing insights.

Surveys can be done through the mail or over the phone, but an increasing number of surveys are using the internet's ability to reach a large number of diverse groups of people.

Interviews

Interviews can take place in research labs, the workplace and even the home. A good interviewer will have extensive training. Many are educated psychologists or anthropologists who understand how to phrase questions, react to answers and gently steer the subject to a particular topic. While interviews lack the sheer numbers of a survey, they do provide depth. A solid research effort will include a large number of interviews of systematically selected people.

Intercepts

An intercept is designed to capitalize on the context and dynamics of a person who is in the midst of a task or action. A typical intercept takes place in a shopping environment where a person is considering purchase decisions. Perceptions, motivations, determining factors, evaluation methods, and more can all be investigated. Intercepts and surveys can be combined in the online world. Sophisticated behavioral targeting can deliver a survey at a precise point to a web user who has followed a particular path or executed a particular set of interactions.

52

Diaries and Journals

Sometimes the best way to gather information about a consumer over time is to let them do it themselves. Journals and diaries are used to let the consumer track their interactions with a brand. Video has added a great new dimension to this technique. Consumers are given video cameras to record their thoughts, brand interactions and contextual information. A researcher can observe an incredible number of subtle cues that a person might never think to jot in a written diary.

Data Mining

Advanced data mining techniques have unlocked a vast amount of brand perception information from email archives, phone call repositories, and web site search engine query databases.

A typical consumer products company might get several thousand emails per month through its web site. Even if the contact form attempts to structure that data or the customer service reps are given the task of categorizing each email as it arrives, much of the meaningful, brand-relevant data may be found in the comments field. Data mining technologies can parse large volumes of email to identify trends and trigger words.

Phone calls offer an additional layer of complexity: since the calls are typically stored as audio files, the data mining systems need to use voice-to-text tools or voice recognition components. Advanced voice data mining systems are able to derive mood, tension and emotion as well as the meaning in the words.

Web site queries are another source of information that is gaining attention. Leading search engines such as Google have created a cultural belief that almost anything can be done through the search field. Consumers visiting a site such as an insurance company web site will put an odd and diverse amount of things into the search field: policy numbers, phone numbers, questions, Social Security numbers - you name it. Mixed in with all of this detritus are good bits of data that indicate the consumers' understanding (or misunderstanding) of the brand.

Undercover Observation

Undercover observation is designed to eliminate the possibility that people will change their behavior when they know that they are being watched or monitored. A manufacturer might work with a retailer to see how users approach store displays. Auto executives might "dress down" and mingle with consumers at a car show. A public relations professional may chat using an alias on internet message boards. The tactic will depend on the type of information desired, privacy policies, and the likelihood of getting accurate, actionable data.

Comparative Associations

Comparative associations allow the research subject to describe the brand by comparing it to different objects, concepts or even people. Typical questions might include, "What type of person do you think would use a product from Brand X?" or "If you could use this brand only once a year, when would it be?" Another might be, "How do you think person A would feel about the product versus person B?" "Describe this brand as an animal." These associations

54

often provide greater detail and meaning than a person can articulate if they are simply asked to describe the brand.

Contextual Analysis

Context analysis can look at physical, emotional, sequential or situational contextual information. One brand of hand tools (hammers, screwdrivers, pliers...) might always be used in the garage or workshop while others might be commonly found in a kitchen drawer. Does this mean one brand is "rugged" and the other is "light duty"? One restaurant might be perceived as a "place to go to celebrate" while another might be "a place to go after a bad day at work." Digging into the context can uncover invaluable information about where a brand lives and potentially powerful associations that can be leveraged.

Brand Removal

Brand removal creates a scenario where research subjects are forced to give up a brand. This removal is an interesting way to find out what the brand truly means to a person. For one brand the response might be, "Truthfully I forgot about it after the first day." While another might be, "I could not believe how much I missed it—I always thought that it was a little important, but now, wow, I can see I really need the product. Using Substitute Z was really no substitute."

Understanding Consumer Perceptions Continues to Evolve

New techniques powered by technology are continually being developed and researchers are blending data from multiple sources within mind-blowing models to produce true consumer insight. For many large companies ongoing consumer brand research is a daily occurrence. Smaller companies often make the mistake of relying on a "feel for the customer" to understand consumer brand perceptions. Research does come at a price, and it does take time. In the end, it is worth it.

Chapter Three

Understanding User Experience, or "UX is the Crux of Slightware"

The world economy is made up of billions of people having experiences with products, places and services.

- People look at packages on a store shelf.

- Enjoy a meal at a restaurant.

- Use an accountant to complete their taxes.

- Visit a resort.

- Read a magazine.

- Browse outfits in a clothing store.

This is the realm of customer experience. As businesses mature, each aspect of the customer experience, called a touch point, is nurtured. This is experience design.

When people use things, and for the purpose of this book, specifically when people use digital things, this is called user experience or UX. The people who shape these interactions are user experience professionals. User experience is not just interface design or writing code. It is the art of understanding people, their needs and abilities. It is also the mastery of processes, methodologies and technologies needed to create digital experiences that deliver success and continually build the brand...not experiences that are slightware.

57

The term can be used in several different ways:

User Experience is a discipline. "That organization has done a good job of including user experience in the overall product offering."

User Experience refers to the complete process of a person using a system. "Checking you 401k account though that web site is not a good user experience."

User Experience can be used as an adjective describing a person's abilities. "He is a seasoned user experience pro."

The acronym "UX" is the go-to shorthand version of the phrase.

Simple enough? You bet, but that doesn't mean companies have developed an appreciation of where good UX can make a difference.

Types of Experiences Where Good UX Can Help Beat Slightware

Businesses are saturated with digital experiences from one end of the enterprise to the other, and consumers are adding digital activities to every part of their lives. Some are out-of-the-box applications that have little room for true UX improvement. Others can be tailored to soundly beat the problem of slightware.

Transactional Experiences

Transactional experiences can be found in ecommerce sites, intranets and extranets. Web users buy products. Employees make charitable contributions. Distributors submit orders.

And on, and on, and on. All of these are transactions. Good user experience improves the conversion rate (the percentage of people who successfully complete a transaction) and can positively impact transaction size and frequency.

Service Applications

The concept of "service" can be applied in many different ways: self service, customer service, employee service and more. By pushing service functions into the digital world companies can realize substantial savings. Done correctly, system usage and user satisfaction soars. Done poorly, companies are forced to maintain costly parallel off-line systems of people, paper and processes.

Purpose-Built Applications

Many devices such as hand-held computers, GPS units, mobile devices and even digital cameras use software applications that marry the functionality of the device with a desktop computer, printer, network or the web. These applications must be easy to use and deliver the utmost confidence. Think of the feeling that consumers have when they first upload digital photos from the camera to the computer, and then are faced with the next step of deleting the images from the camera. Wow—they want to be SURE that the images are REALLY on the computer. Purpose-built applications typically use a fixed set of input devices (think of the buttons/settings on the camera), but have ability to use an application as a bridge to more complex functionality and future enhancements. Shoot the photo - upload the photo - retouch the photo - send to Grandma. Perfect! A great, understood and satisfying user experience.

59

Integrated Applications

The ability to effectively use a device has an enormous impact on the perception of the brand. Unlike purpose-built applications, integrated applications are not created with changes or enhancements in mind. Coffeemakers, microwaves, televisions and other devices have interfaces, input devices, and software-powered functionality that deliver value but remain relatively fixed over time. As engineers and product designers imagine new features, a UX pro should consider the ability of the user to effectively use the device. So...the new XYZ microwave can change its power setting according to a user-programmed schedule to deliver a tastier treat! Yes, the microwave *can,* but is the user able to figure out *how* to enter those settings? Or the classic: Check into a hotel and attempt to set the alarm on an unfamiliar alarm clock. It *should* be simple.

Learning Applications

Education via all forms of digital experiences is destined to expand. Universities can offer courses to geographically diverse students. Companies can continually on-board new employees rather than waiting for periodically scheduled training programs. Elementary schools can put students on individual tracks rather than forcing teachers to teach to the top, middle or bottom of a class. These systems are usually defined by the environment or system (this is the part that keeps track of students, their courses, progress, etc.) and the actual learning experiences (courses now include virtual discussions, team projects via chat, online testing, etc.) The systems and the construction of the courses need to feel almost invisible. The student and teacher should be able to focus on the material, rather than spending time wrestling with software.

60

Twenty-five years from now students won't gripe about a miserable teacher. They will besmirch a poorly executed online learning experience.

Business Communication

Brands need to communicate with employees, stock holders, investors, analysts, regulators, the media, business partners, board members, and many other audiences. As Marshall McLuhan said, "The medium is the message." Consider annual reports, press conferences, financial releases and recruitment campaigns. Each has always been viewed as a distinct, thoughtful, and carefully constructed art form. These communications are now being turned into digital experiences. Can a recent college graduate with a programming degree execute an online annual report with the same level of polish, intuition and appeal as an Art Director who has been doing annual reports for 20 years? No, probably not. Can a seasoned PR pro create all of the technical documentation needed by the IT department to build an online event? Again, the answer is no. Business communicators and UX pros need to collaborate to harness the possibilities and limitations of the digital space. Could animation help that chart? Should this screen be printable? Can a person extract this information from a restricted access site and forward it?

With business communications done well, companies look informed and smart. Done poorly — they don't.

Social and Community Experiences

Social and community functions can be as large as complete sites like Facebook, or as small as a simple product rating on a web site. In either case they allow people to shape the dialogue around brands. UX pros and brand professionals need to define the agenda around these functions as well as understand the social norms within the internet community. Most companies have not formulated a policy around something as simple as negative product reviews on their own web sites. Some companies would remove them immediately, while others might hope that the positive reviews outweigh the negative ones. Some might hope a balance of positive and negative reviews builds credibility. Other companies simply avoid the situation altogether by not enabling reviews. Imagine the user reaction to a revelation that reviews were being omitted or altered. Now *that's* digital brand damage.

Information and Data Display

The world is awash in information. The web and blogs make news almost instantaneous, and company systems record incredible amounts of data. Relational data can be presented and analyzed in numerous ways through application interfaces. Executives now use real-time dashboards to monitor the health and reputation of a company. Information, though, does not always have meaning. It is not the same as intelligence. Good user experience is essential for adding value to the way people access and use information.

Music, Pictures and Media

A point to ponder:

From this very point in time, the ability of mankind to <u>create</u> will only increase.

Kenneth J. Weiss

Powerful. Kinda fun, too. Cell phones have cameras. Off-the-shelf computers include video, audio and photo editing programs. Web sites will store files for free. Free! Home printers are delivering unbelievable quality. Imagine the stuff that hasn't even hit the market yet! Wow.

So, how does a user capture, edit, store, organize, share and even create revenue from this? How do communities give all of this content meaning? How is ownership monitored? Can it be? How do files jump between devices? Amazing questions. "Accidental" user experiences won't work, and in many instances the experience design is as critical as the device.

Added Dimensions

Every one of these user experiences can be accentuated and augmented with additional dimensions.

Mobile

All types of experiences are being pushed to the mobile world. Data delivery rates are different, input devices are different, and interface sizes are different. But people are increasingly taking their digitized lives on-the-go.

Mashed

Want to make an experience more valuable? Combine it with other experiences. Mashups are the chocolate and peanut butter of the digital world. Separate, good. Together, mmmmm.

Widget

Widgets are small little user experiences that are created to exist within other environments. Widgets can be found on desktops, in large social networks and embedded in other applications. Ding from Southwest was a pioneer, and hundreds of other companies wrapped up brands and functions into widgets and apps for properties like Facebook. The UX for a widget is very different: less screen real estate, a tighter set of input functions, a narrower focus and a belief that a brand can be built without monopolizing a person's attention or time.

Open

In order to increase the odds of a user experience succeeding, it is often created in an open format so that others may build upon it. This often supercharges the adoption of viable experiences, and helps them work their way into untapped segments of a market, or even into completely new markets. What will ultimately happen to the experience? Hard to say. But opening an experience is a risk, and a possible reward for brands.

Socialized

Social experiences are some of the hottest properties of Web 2.0. The basic idea is inherently brilliant: Create something that lots of people will use and talk about. *Voila!* Instant audiences with demographic information and mounds of behavioral data. Not only do they become incredibly powerful brands, but they are also a magnet for other brands looking to connect with a particular audience segment. Downside? The community is in control. People can say anything and they sometimes use the most, uh, colorful language. The brand of the social experience itself can be drastically recast by the community and participating brands are often only a few clicks away from all sorts of content.

And Gaming Ups the Bar

The computing power of game systems is incredible. So good in fact, that the technology makes national security types squeamish. Take the system and play the newest first person shooter or mod it to make the ultimate hacking tool. Ah, decisions... In any event, game systems and game culture are dramatically reshaping the universe. Think of the kid who plays games. The typical game allows them to switch vantage points, see real time status for their character, peek at a competitor's characters, preview what might be around the corner, etc. Advanced sound design not only creates mood, but also provides detailed feedback and serves as a storyline. What will these users expect from interfaces of the future?

The Fuzzy Edges of UX

Users follow circuitous paths from the real world to the digital world and back. They even can exist with one foot in both. Ever talked to a company on the 800 number while staring at their web site? A perfect example. These paths can be broken down into simple building blocks.

Clicks

Transactions in the online world. Typically some form of conversion such as completing a sale, signing up for a newsletter, or downloading a file.

Bricks

Activity in the physical, offline world such as a store purchase or visit.

Tips

Inspired by the old ad slogan, "Let Your Finger(tip)s Do the Walking." *Tips* is using the phone to connect.

Flips

Offline paper catalogs.

Picks

Researching and deciding on a product via one channel, but moving to another to complete the transaction.

These can be assembled in almost any order:

A user makes a purchase on a web site and picks up the item at the store = Clicks and Bricks.

A user researches a product on a manufacturer's web site and then jumps to a retailer web site to complete the purchase = Picks and Clicks.

A person browses a catalog and then completes the sale at the web site = Flips and Clicks.

Solid, informed, validated and tested user experience is the key to beating slightware in today's multi-channel world.

Kenneth J. Weiss

The Dynamics of Copy and Content in Digital Experiences

Is writing for digital experiences different from writing for other types of communication? Absolutely. Radio scripts don't work well on TV. Call center operators do not read the text from print ads. Copy and content, at their best, are crafted specifically for the digital medium. Creators need to know how to make it right, and what might go wrong.

First, What Makes Good Content?

Writing for digital experiences including web sites, CD-ROMs, kiosks, etc. is a distinct art. The flows within experiences may be different and the objectives of the experiences may be different, so "good" is contextual. However, some basic rules of thumb provide an initial means of evaluation.

Inverted Pyramid

The inverted pyramid is a concept borrowed from journalism: Structure the content so the lead paragraph tells the complete story (who, what, where, when and why). Follow that with a deeper dive into the details. This makes experiences much more usable, and recognizes the fact that the path though an experience is not always linear. Users can view pages or screens, read the first paragraph, and then decide whether or not to read the details.

Benefits First

Placing the benefits first is one of the toughest principles for traditionally trained copywriters to follow. On the web, the benefit should come first and the rationale (the features that provide the benefit) should come second. This is counter to decades of traditional advertising thinking.

Here's a traditional marketing paragraph:

Integrity, honesty and personal accountability are the guiding principles of <insert company name>. Our one hundred years of dealing with customers is a testament to this approach. For you, our valued customer, this means one thing: you can trust us with your <money, investments, legal affairs, yada yada yada>.

It feels traditional because it has been written hundreds, if not thousands, of times. The reader needs to churn through all of the copy just to get to the benefit. It may be lyrical but it is hardly efficient.

Digital experiences demand that the benefit be placed first because users want to execute tasks quickly. Efficiency is paramount!

A better digital paragraph would be:

Above all else, customers can trust us with <whatever>. We've earned this trust day after day for over one hundred years, and we'll earn your trust everyday with our guiding principles of integrity, honesty and personal accountability.

The benefits-first approach is essential for all types of products and services. In a time-starved attention-shortened world, long, rambling paragraphs will be abandoned.

This approach is often a difficult sell for tenured marketers. It is so different that it feels wrong, but it is actually incredibly right for digital experiences.

The Less/More Arrangement

Larger pieces of content such as articles, white papers, editorials, How-To's, guides, etc. should be constructed with a short version supported by a longer version. A user can breeze through the short form and then decide if they want greater depth. An alternative, equally successful arrangement is a short version supported by a series of content chunks that dive deeper into each particular aspect of the piece. A web page dealing with Sherman's march through Georgia could be led with a solid article covering the big picture and then be followed by a series of articles covering the agricultural aftermath, political implications, military significance, and effects on southern architecture. Such an arrangement is far more usable and digestible than a single article attempting to cover all of the subject matter. The supporting articles also benefit from the ability to be connected thematically to similar pieces.

Typography in Sync with Usability

Imagine if a person writing copy for the site decided that underlining the key points of a paragraph was the best way to highlight their significance. The poor user would, of course, come along and try to click on each one. This is a very obvious conflict between typography and usability, but more subtle instances of italics, color treatment, placement and text executed as a graphic can cause similar problems.

Experiences need to maintain a rigorous set of rules for the treatment of copy, headlines, subheads, form labels, instructions and error messages to maximize usability.

Restrained Use of Internal Links

Internal links are links that are interspersed within paragraphs of copy designed to give users a shortcut to related content. Internal links are an element of good search engine optimization, and when used in moderation can be helpful to readers. When used too frequently, the readability of the paragraph is hampered and the user is not given a clear sense of what might be really important because almost everything is made to look really important.

Enough White Space

User experiences offer an incredible amount of scalability and screen real estate—so, of course, people want to fill up every last pixel! White space, the visual breathing room within an interface, helps users separate content, identify relationships and understand levels of importance. Generally, white space makes the experience easier to digest. Include it at all costs.

Scannable

Good, explanatory headlines, subheads and title elements are essential for making an interface easy to scan. Unlike traditional forms of communication that do not require a subhead for every new paragraph, interfaces are greatly enhanced with structured headlines, subheads and text along with titles for images, charts and other graphics. These give users the ability to quickly scan the interface, understand each part, and then determine where to invest additional time.

Good Printability

Interface screens and web pages that are printable (or those with a print-formatted counterpart) provide something incredibly valuable for user experiences: hard transmission. A good printable page leaps from the digital world into the physical world, providing the opportunity for permanence.

The screen that prints, but cuts off the right hand edge of all the sentences, gets thrown away. The screen that prints but superimposes black bars over spaces is an annoyance. The screen that prints but fails to carry a brand reference or clear indication of how to visit that screen or page again is a wasted opportunity.

Avoiding Vernacular as Navigation

Any discussion of navigation really belongs in a review of Information Architecture, but content people are often called upon to "organize" the web site or other user experience. One of the most problematic mistakes is the use of company or industry vernacular as navigation. Imagine going to the web site of a company that makes lawn tractors. The navigation gives three options: "The 300 Series," "The 700 Series" and "The 1200 Series." Sure, that's how *the company* thinks about the product lines, but those labels mean nothing to the user. Nothing! Even vernacular that is slightly more descriptive may still be unclear if the users are unfamiliar with the product category.

Audience Appropriate

Content must be created for the target audience. That is a reasonable rule to grasp. In the hyper-segmented online world, however, audiences can spot an outsider a mile away. They know who "gets" their world. They know who

71

is just pretending. The content standards of informed depth and accuracy are pushed higher everyday. And...these audiences tend to have rapidly changing terminology and pop-cultural standards. Easy, huh?

Brand Approved

Brand standards for the correct use of brand names, approved phrases and "no-nos" are as old as the oldest profession's use of the phrase, "Hey fella, looking for a good time?" (An industry approved update of, "Would you fancy some company?" See, with on-brand messaging the market knows exactly what you mean.) The ease of digital publishing means that brand standards for copy should be closely policed. Unlike previous decades where catalogs and sell sheets were only created periodically, today's businesses create market-facing communications on a daily basis. So, who's watching the brand? Are the content creators trained brand communicators?

Search Engine Friendly

Search engines need to be considered as an audience for web sites. High search engine rankings are paramount for many companies, and as such, the approach to content needs to accommodate the strange and fickle algorithms of search engines. (Note: Search engine optimization is a challenging, ongoing activity that requires years of observation and experimentation. This little paragraph will not make you an expert.) So, what do search engines look for? Lots of stuff, including all types of visible and hidden characteristics of individual pages. Search engines also look at how a web site relates to the rest of the internet and how it is referenced on other sites. When it comes to text, search engines look for which words and phrases are used. If the site refers

72

to a product in a particular way, but the market calls it something different, search engines may identify the match, but not rank it highly. Similarly, search engines will work through differences in spelling and terminology, but rankings will suffer. Search engines examine the placement and format of text along with word order. Density (how often a word appears) and thematic consistency (the number of topics within the context of a page or site) also play a role. Great, search engine friendly copy is best left to the experts, but they need to be involved in projects from the beginning. SEO, search engine optimization, is not frosting that can be slathered on a half-baked cake.

How Digital Systems Affect Copy, Images and Other Content

The creation of good content is an investment, and companies naturally want to leverage that investment by re-using content in multiple venues. This is affectionately referred to as "repurposing." When not done carefully, a number of potential snafus can damage the UX and the brand.

Broken Spatial Relationships

When copy moves from an offline realm into the digital world it often brings spatial references. Newspaper articles may include a line that says "See accompanying story on the left." Or, "See story below." Even if the complementary element joins the source content on the digital journey, it may not be positioned "on the left," or "below," etc. Manual editing solves this problem, but more copy is being pulled dynamically into web sites on a daily basis from other sources without human-eyeball-oversight.

Broken Content Relationships

Copy often carries relationships with images, graphics, references and other pieces of copy. A passage from a textbook could include the phrase "...one of our founding fathers, George Washington, pictured here, was renowned for his ability to..." Much like spatial relationships, the integrity of these types of references may not remain intact in all digital systems.

Broken Linearity

Imagine a paragraph of copy that starts, "As we mentioned before..." Such an introduction might make sense to a person reading the middle article in a series of articles. It makes no sense if it leads a page on a web site that a user has never previously visited. (Such as a person following a link from Google that lands them on a lower level page.) These types of phrases make sense when the format of the experience guarantees linearity or imposes a strict sequence, but in many UX instances, these will conflict with the users' actual paths.

Context Removal

One of the downsides of a cut-and-paste world is that small chunks of content can be plucked from a source independently of their surrounding context. Unlike broken spatial relationships and broken content relationships, the fundamental meaning of an element can be changed by removing its context. This happens frequently with sound bites from interviews and also occurs with images, video clips, charts, data points and more.

Truncation

When content is dynamically placed in digital systems, all sorts of weirdness happens where big content elements are squeezed into small digital holes. Job titles with too many characters are shortened, large chunks of headlines are lopped off, pictures are squished and cropped, and even entire paragraphs of text are vaporized.

Odd Line Breaks

It's amazing how line breaks can make a sentence great

ly change its meaning.

Dynamic content within digital experiences often suffers from this mistake.

Content Scraping

Most digital content is highly portable. Automated scripts and crawlers can be created to scrape content from web sites. Some legitimate uses for these techniques do exist but often content-scraping is done by the ne'er-do-wells of the world. Content is scraped from sites, loaded into a tangle of pages, and used to scam search engines for higher organic listings. Scraped content can also be used to create a web site around a particular topic. Once the "site" is created, the owner signs up to have a search engine's paid listings appear on the pages. The site feels real enough for the search engine, and the paid search listings are fed to the site. The site owner can then commit click fraud by repeatedly clicking on the listings.

Multi-Source Juxtaposition

New technologies are allowing content to be dynamically collected from multiple sources and displayed within a single interface: News and entertainment sites merge content from numerous streams. Industry web sites aggregate information from a variety of sources. Retailer sites receive product feeds from vendors and insert user comments from other sources. Corporate intranets and extranets pull information from divergent internal and external sources. The mixing gets more complex as advertising and promotional messages are interjected into the experience. The problem can be further compounded when users are given the ability to personalize the experience.

The intent of combining the content is to offer a deeper and wider user experience, but content conflicts do arise.

- An advertisement for minivans is placed on a news site within a story about a minivan crash

- The welcome screen of a company intranet announces a series of promotions in the senior ranks while at the same time featuring an industry research report about shrinking sales.

- Competitive products appear on a retailers site next to each other with contradictory marketing statements.

Such problems are challenging to the user since the sources are invisible to the point that the user perceives only ONE source. "Wow," the user says, "I can't believe that the site says that *and* that!" The risk is that brands wind up looking silly and insensitive.

Multi-Source Formatting Errors

When content is brought from multiple sources, it usually comes with some amount of formatting. Fonts, the use of italics, size, etc., are easy to strip out or normalize, but other, more subtle formatting elements are more elusive. Product nomenclature inconsistencies, capitalization issues, the uses of dashes and other issues are all more difficult to identify and standardize on the fly.

Multi-Source Style and Tonality Issues

Warm-and-friendly, meet bold-and-authoritative! Brand voice is difficult for business people to capture in their communications and content. The sales team might describe a product powerfully! Lots of incredible, descriptive, and powerful adjectives! The customer service group may take a more thoughtful, parsed route when explaining a product. Imagine how this content looks combined within a single digital experience. The brand voice takes life as a Robin Williams routine.

Multi-Source Audience Errors

Think of the "About Us" section of a large publicly traded company's web site. The content is most likely the convergence of content originally targeted for investors, analysts, business partners, the press, current employees, potential employees and other groups. Some of the content will stay aligned with that audience, and other copy may bleed across audiences while carrying its original slant.

For instance, within a company, multiple versions of its history exist as copy. Sounds odd, but it is true. Human Resources will have a version of its history for new and prospective employees. Investor Relations has a version

77

that focuses on the business dynamics of the company's past. The public relations department typically has a version that serves as background information for journalists. Other versions exist as well. Once copy is dumped into the hopper of a digital experience, the intended audience can become disconnected from the copy. No finger-pointing here, but plenty of web sites have corporate histories in their careers sections that feature odd phrases like, "as part of the company's recapitalization plan early in 2001..." That is a great bit of information for the investment community—but probably not relevant to the person who wants a job in the customer service department.

Typos and Grammar

Digital technologies have greatly contributed to the decentralized creation of copy, but effective editing has not been decentralized with the same success. Spell-check may catch some problems. Not all. Grammar issues can, and do, make it through. As more people are granted content creation and publishing authority, the odds of typos and grammar problems increase.

In the old days there was intense scrutiny of copy when a TV spot was produced for airing on local television (let alone a national TV campaign). Now that after-the-fact editing is possible, people are slightly less vigilant.

Factual Errors and Downright Fiction for Fun and Fraud

Digital experiences and the web, in particular, have the ability to make things look "real." Little bits of satirical text are sometimes confused with the truth, because the presentation is so real. (Ever read theonion.com?) Generally these bits are all in good fun, but sometimes turn up in an email as

78

"OMG, I just saw that Kansas is going to secede from the USA!" Unfortunately this email lands next to the one that says, "There is a problem with your checking account, please log in here to update your information" - a scam designed to fool people into divulging sensitive personal information that can lead to fraud or identity theft.

Opinion/Fact Blending

Want to read a good product review? Skilled and experienced editors write reviews. The casual user writes reviews. Even the presidents of companies and marketing managers review their own products in blogs. So where is the line between fact and opinion? Is it different in every instance? Absolutely. The challenging part for users is that all sources can appear to have the same level of professionalism. Thanks to the simplicity of a cut-and-paste world, reviews from a variety of sources may all have the same product glamour shots, usage shots and supporting documentation.

Time References

The web has lots of dusty corners, and even practiced user experience professionals sometimes lose track of what was said when.

"It's hard to believe it's been five years since we've moved into our new building." Oops. They moved into that building in 1995. The web page was published in 2000 but never updated.

"We believe in innovation—just wait until you see what we have planned for 2002."

These types of time references would be understandable if they were only found in date-context vehicles like press releases. Unfortunately they can be found on very important

79

pages of web sites—even, *gasp*, the home page. Time references also come in the form of style, fashion and other visual cues. Hey, how old is that picture of the CFO? He still
had hair!

Legal Precedent and Problems

If a statement is made on a web site, is it the same as making
a promise in an advertisement? When does a line of copy
become a legal obligation? When does an employee's response to a blog posting become legally binding? Can the
CEO of a publicly traded company blog at will without
treading outside the lines drawn by the SEC? What are the
ramifications of outdated copy remaining on a web site?
When do marketing statements become comparative claims
that require substantiation?

Digital experiences make publishing easy, and make legal
counsel nervous.

So What's the Remedy?

Getting content right is tricky and the standards for quality
seem to be dipping. Users are more forgiving of errors (but
hey may hold you to the letter of the copy if it is in their best
interest) and the ability to edit in the digital world has made
companies and brands less vigilant. Imagine if every web
page was scrutinized the same way a brochure was before a
printing press belched out 25,000 copies. Content may be
more accurate but speed would suffer.

What to do? What to do? Companies need clear channels of
feedback, available resources for editing, widely distributed
visual and editorial style guides, agreed upon vocabularies,
an institutional commitment to quality, clear content owner-

80

ship, and rock solid work flows—nothing will undo good work and goodwill like having multiple people making changes to multiple versions of a file.

In a perfect world every content element is proofed for grammatical errors, double checked for factual accuracy and judged against brand and style considerations. This should happen every time content is created, reviewed periodically when it is digitized and continually scrutinized for the problems of existing in a digital world.

Innovations and Artifacts, The Devices That Empower Users Within Experiences

An ever-shifting spectrum of devices used for interaction, orientation and assistance can be found within user experiences. At one end, artifacts: culturally understood mechanisms. At the other, innovations: concepts designed to differentiate while providing utility.

If an experience is infused with innovations the user could be pleasantly surprised or hopelessly confused. Conversely, if the experience relies completely on artifacts the user will most likely execute a task flawlessly, though the advanced user could find the experience pedantic.

Impact

Impact is a measure of an item's contribution to the success of all user experiences. Some, like tabs, are an invaluable means of grouping content. Others, such as check boxes and

Innovations & Artifacts in The User Experience

by Kenneth J. Weiss

Artifact

Impact

Obsolescence

Blue Hyperlinks
Check Boxes
Upper Left Home
"X" Means Close
Radio Buttons
Drop Down Menus
Text Fields
Home/Back/More/Here
Tabs
Drop Down Boxes
Left Section Navigation
Footer Links
Top Global Navigation
Active, Inactive, Rollover & Expired
Plus Sign
Scroll Bars
File Link Labels
Magnifying Glass
Color Palette Strategy
Tree Menus
Structured Writing - Size & Indents
Gripper Textures
The Arrow
Drag and Drop Navigation
Tool Tips
Bread Crumb Navigation
Slideshow Controls
Video Player Controls
Audio/No Audio Icon
Device Styling for Navigation
Floating Layers
Expandable Areas
Sliders
Modular Containers
Window Shades/Accordions
Chicklets
Expanding/Reactive Menus
Image Scrollers
Docking
Zooming Visual Menus
Sequential Panels
3D Navigation Systems

Scrolling Text
Fly Out Menus
The Animated Arrow
Frames Based Navigation
Under Construction Graphic
Animated Mail Envelopes
Bad Iconography
Flames, Blinking and Spinning
Beveled Buttons
Single Image Navigation
Animated Bullets
Marble Buttons
Physical Object Metaphors For Navigation
Physical Space Metaphors for Navigation
Welcome to My Home Page
Spider Webs
Globes

Innovation

www.Slightware.com

This infographic is governed by the Creative Commons Attribution-Non-Commercial ShareAlike 2.5 License. creativecommons.org

(cc) SOME RIGHTS RESERVED

radio buttons, are the workhorses of experiences, but could be used interchangeably.

Obsolescence

Ideas that come into vogue, enjoy some usage, but never quite secure a foothold in the vernacular of user experience fall to the realm of obsolescence. Long-tenured web users remember when marble buttons and giant image maps once powered navigation, communication and basic transactions.

Picking a Spot on the Continuum

The decisions of whether, and how, to mix innovations and artifacts is essential in the artful creation of every user experience. Entertainment, fashion, and cutting-edge brands as well as brands with agile, imaginative audiences can more heavily utilize innovations. The web sites of banks, insurance companies, etc., require the user to have a high degree of confidence as they interact, so incorporating artifacts is important.

Movement Along the Continuum

Not all innovations evolve into artifacts. Some are undermined by better technology. Some are corrected though common sense and user feedback. Others would have been better left as a layer in the Photoshop file.

In the Skin

Any innovation or artifact can be skinned in different ways. The skin is the look and feel of the elements including the colors, textures, dimensional treatments, and behaviors. Any innovation or artifact can be improved or harmed by the design of the skin.

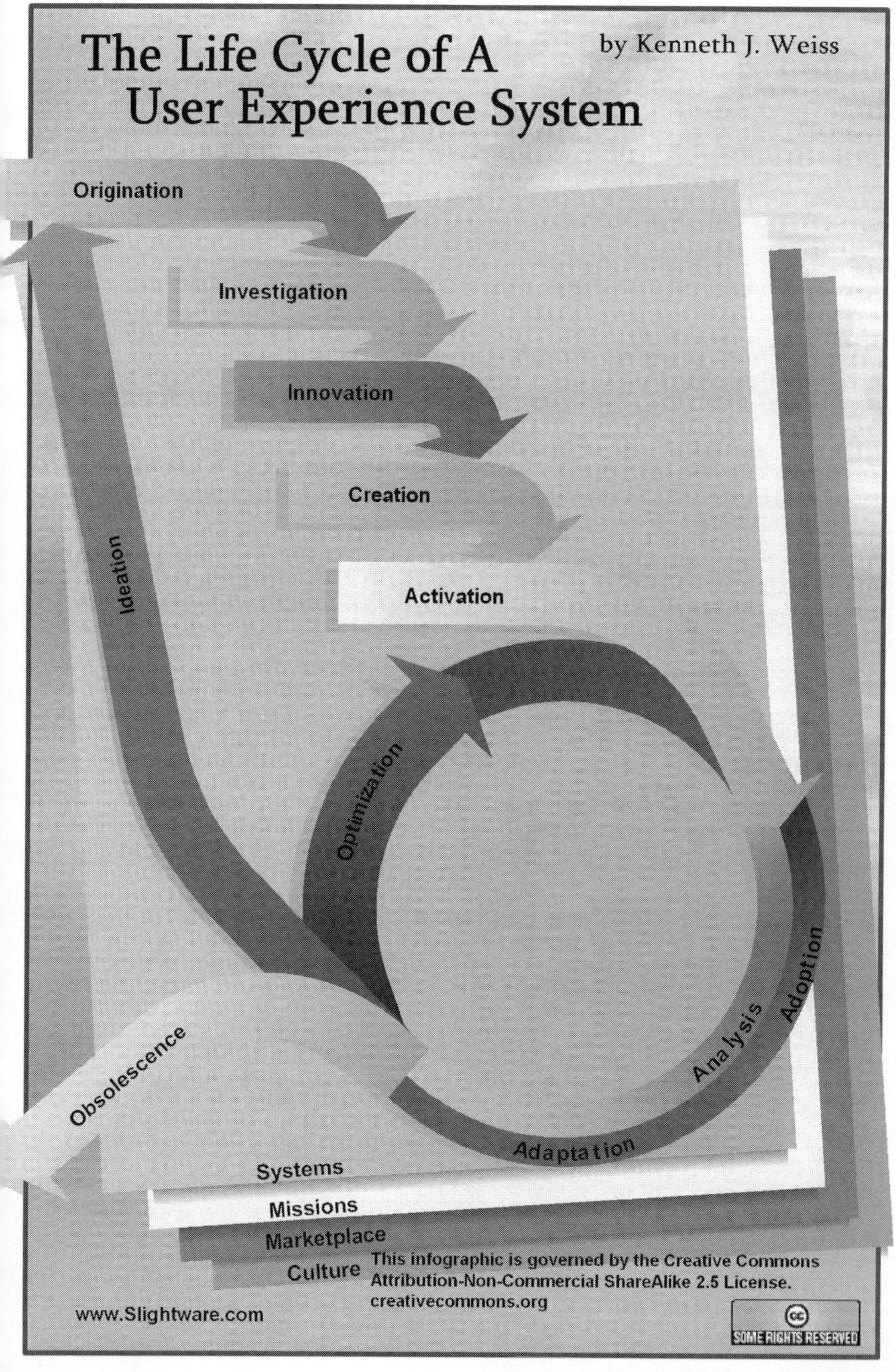
The Life Cycle of A User Experience System
by Kenneth J. Weiss
Origination
Investigation
Innovation
Creation
Activation
Ideation
Optimization
Adoption
Analysis
Adaptation
Obsolescence
Systems
Missions
Marketplace
Culture
This infographic is governed by the Creative Commons Attribution-Non-Commercial ShareAlike 2.5 License. creativecommons.org
www.Slightware.com
SOME RIGHTS RESERVED

The User Experience Lifecycle

New user experiences are being created everyday. Each experience powered by hardware and software follows a similar path from inception to incapacitation, or to reincarnation. User experience pros and brand advocates need to mindfully drive this process rather than just let it happen. This is more than project management. It is an informed approach to strategically guiding UX efforts.

Origination

The spark! It may ignite from within the organization, or from research, or from user feedback. It can even spring from one thoughtful mind alone. Great origination feels fresh, promising and sometimes incredibly obvious.

Investigation

Is it possible? Does the market need it? Who will build it? Where will it live? Are there legal considerations? Disheartening answers should not always stop the process.

Innovation

This is the step that separates vision from folly. The scope and requirements are established within the constraints of time and costs in the form of detailed documents. These documents serve as the blueprints that shows how great the experience may be.

Creation

The complete development process including the dozens and dozens of little decisions that make the project better as the build is executed.

85

Activation

Activation is not simply a "go live" moment. It is the launch of the system in concert with awareness and adoption programs to establish connectivity with the target.

Adoption

The target audience begins to use the experience! Sometimes as designed, sometimes in a different way. How often, in how many instances, all of the features, or just a few?

Analysis

Initial excitement must be tempered with impartial measurement. Are the intended consequences occurring? Are unintended consequences happening? Are there downstream ripples, and what is happening at varying degrees of separation?

Adaptation

The system flexes to meet the user. This is natural movement within the usage of the system: users add content, submit questions, etc. Additional phases, functions, or data sources come online. Additional hardware or connectivity might be added.

Optimization

Once the system has reached an initial point of stasis, smart tweaks can be made to improve conversion, drive ROI or even lower the total cost of ownership.

Obsolescence

Sadly, the system fades away. Changes in business objectives, new technologies, shifting consumer preferences and competitive activities can precipitate the end.

Ideation

The experience of building the system and the knowledge gained throughout the lifecycle lead to a new frame of reference which fosters fresh ideas.

So Where Does It Happen?

Even the most basic brands and organizations share common contexts.

Systems

These include technical environments, organizational systems, and business processes.

Missions

"Mission statements" go in and out of vogue, but organizations and business have cumulative and individual forces that make the entity tick.

Marketplace

Good user experiences satisfy a need within a traditional marketplace or the marketplace of advocacy and loyalty.

Culture

Culture is the shared world as it spills into the future and into the past, across groups and boundaries.

The User Experience Funnel

by Kenneth J. Weiss

Generated Users

Serendipitous Users

Self-Directed Users

Online Touches

Offline Touches

Sponsor's Imperceptible Goals

Sponsor's Perceptible Goals

The Desired User Experience

The Intended User Experience

The Tangible Layer

The Intangible Layer

Outcomes

The Actual User Experience

This infographic is governed by the Creative Commons Attribution-Non-Commercial ShareAlike 2.5 License.
creativecommons.org

SOME RIGHTS RESERVED

www.Slightware.com

The User Experience Funnel

User experiences include a wide range of interactions powered by software such as web site visits, chat interactions, phone calls, the use of self-service kiosks, and more. All of these experiences share a similar flow with common user types.

Generated Users

Users driven to the experience by any communication or effort are generated users. These specific users may or may not have participated in the experience at all without those communications.

Self-Directed Users

Users who find their own way to the experience are self-directed. While some amount of brand awareness, insight or previous experience might be at play, generally these users' tasks, needs and ambitions are responsible for leading them to the experience.

Serendipitous Users

Users who accidentally encounter the experience are serendipitous users.

Online Touches

Wired touches such as email or chat can drive traffic, set expectations and structure the entrance to a system.

Offline Touches

Touches such as paper mail or advertising create awareness and deliver brand messages. Extensions for phone numbers, vanity URLs and the famous ".com/campaign" can be used to direct a person to a specific experience.

Sponsor's Perceptible Goals

Sponsors not only want to satisfy needs, but also position their brands, sell more, collect information and generate additional use. These goals are often evident to the user.

Sponsor's Imperceptible Goals

Sponsors also have goals that are not evident to the user. These goals, such as dropping a cookie, recording behavioral information or collecting personal data for later resale may even be objectionable to the user.

The Tangible Layer

Some elements of the experience are very apparent to the user, including the interface, copy or audio.

The Intangible Layer

Largely unknown to the user is a deep intangible layer which includes the many background systems that shape, monitor, and record the experience.

The Intended User Experience

User experiences have intended outcomes by design. The ideal experience from the sponsor's perspective is an experience where both the perceptible and the imperceptible goals are met.

The Desired User Experience

Users have an ideal experience in mind when entering any user experience. This may include maintaining anonymity,

90

executing the experience in a short period of time, or disclosing minimal information.

The Actual User Experience

This is the experience as viewed by an objective party. Some level of success may be enjoyed by the sponsor and user, or neither.

Outcomes

User experiences generate vast amounts of data. "Perfect" data would show a clear, clean finish for the user and sponsor. In reality the data is muddy. The residual elements of the experience can include "to-do's" such as the need for additional interaction, channel switching, or further actions to improve the odds of retention.

Campaigns vs. Conversations

Traditional marketing has been demarcated by periods known as campaigns. Campaigns were typically aligned around sales seasons, product launches and responses to market forces. Campaign-based thinking allowed for periods of strategy, execution and measurement. Good campaign management brought rapid cycle times.

Conversations are beautifully amorphous and adaptable with fundamentally different dynamics. By understanding the possibilities of software, campaign thinking changes to good conversation. An examination of campaigns and these new conversations shows distinct differences.

91

Campaigns
Versus
Conversations

by Kenneth J. Weiss

Characteristics of Campaigns

Characteristics of Conversations

User Has Little Input in Conclusion

Conclusion Based on Resolution

Based Upon Context Snapshot

Based Upon Actual Context

Purposed for Time Frame

Purposed in Real Time

Generalized Approach

Approach Matches Need

Segmented

Hyper-Segmented

Periodic

Continuous

This infographic is governed by the Creative Commons Attribution-Non-Commercial ShareAlike 2.5 License.
creativecommons.org

www.Slightware.com

SOME RIGHTS RESERVED

User Has Little Input on Conclusion / Conclusion Based on Resolution

The close of a campaign is typically instigated by the sponsor. Sometimes measurements indicate that the campaign has been successful or is failing to have the desired effect. Other times the constraints of cost and logistics bring about a prescribed end. The close of a conversation, however, is controlled by the user. Software allows for a low-cost/no-cost dialogue that can follow myriad paths and draw to a natural end when a resolution ultimately occurs.

Based Upon Context Snapshot / Based Upon Actual Context

Production lead times create a dissonance between the observed situation and the audience's exposure to the campaign. Simply put: Campaigns take some amount of production time. Ideally the snapshot of the context is viable when the campaign runs. If not, the campaign fails or addresses an irrelevant situation. In conversations the context is continually sampled to make sure it is viable.

Purposed for Time Frame / Purposed in Real Time

In campaigns the purpose is usually tied to some time frame, and each campaign has a limited number of purposes known as goals and objectives. Within a conversation, the purpose exists in real time and can evolve or change. Think of the phone call that can change the tasks ahead when the rep says, "And is there anything else I can help you with?"

Generalized Approach / Approach Matches Needs

Different members of a target audience might respond to different messages, types of communication, timing, im-

93

Slightware - The Next Great Threat to Brands

agery, etc. Campaigns, however, cannot address each nuance and instead take a generalized, although honed when possible, approach. Conversations are completely adaptive and use an approach that matches the needs and biases of the target.

Segmented / Hyper-Segmented

Campaigns are designed to reach defined audiences. An audience can be targeted by any number of traditional and emerging attributes, but at some point, targeting smaller audiences becomes cost-prohibitive. Software brings amazing efficiencies that allow conversations to occur with incredibly small target audiences—right down to a one-to-one conversation.

Periodic / Continuous

Campaigns by their very nature have starting and stopping points. Conversations are continuous and flow uninterrupted from one to the next.

UX – Just Getting Started

Human Computer Interaction and Human Factors have long track records of investigating the way people use devices and accomplish processes. UX is just getting started. Articles, whitepapers, research projects and books are invaluable, but none will replace the experience of working on dozens if not hundreds of projects. Experiment. Learn. Document. Share. Teach. The advancement of the field is the responsibility of every person who practices UX.

94

Chapter Four

The Causes of Slightware

Creating great user experiences that build brands is difficult. Every user experience should be great. Users should not just be satisfied. They should be ecstatic. Brands should be exalted. Yeah, well, it doesn't always happen that way. Why not? Within companies, brand, IT, and corporate constituencies generate palpable friction. Other operations, information, technology and cultural forces may be somewhat more removed, but just as damaging.

Experience Forces vs. Brand Forces

Experience and brand forces work in opposition within the user experience. Rarely do they find a perfect balance. These conflicting forces arise early in requirements, fester during development, and compete for user's attention during the lifespan of the experience. For each of the following sub-heads, the user experience force is listed first followed by the contradicting slightware force.

Familiar vs. Unique

Good usability dictates that conventions which are known and understood by users should be employed while brand strategy places a premium on being unique.

Clarity Driven vs. Personality Driven

In order for labels and copy within experiences to optimally help the user they must be driven by clarity. Brands, however, desire a distinct personality and voice.

by Kenneth J. Weiss

Experience Forces
Versus Brand Forces

Toward The Ideal User Experience

Experience Forces

Brand Forces

Familiar

Unique

Clarity Driven

Personality Driven

Understandable

Engaging

Transferable

Ownable

Predictable

Differentiating

Task Centric

Conveyance Centric

Finite

Lasting

This infographic is governed by the Creative Commons Attribution-Non-Commercial ShareAlike 2.5 License. creativecommons.org

SOME RIGHTS RESERVED

www.Slightware.com

Understandable vs. Engaging

Users typically want experiences that are immediately clear and intuitive while brands tend to seek immersion and longer periods of involvement.

Transferable vs. Ownable

Good user experiences help the user build a collective knowledge of how systems in general work and behave. Brands like to singularly own feelings, emotions, and a position in the mind.

Predictable vs. Differentiating

Users are more comfortable within experiences that act in predictable ways. Predictability provides ongoing affirmation and comfort. Brands by nature want to stand apart with each step in the interaction revealing something new, desirable, and different.

Task Centric vs. Conveyance Centric

In some instances, the user experience is built solely to help the user execute a task: usability is key. Brands, on the contrary, prefer experiences where not only is the task executed but a message or concept is also instilled within the user.

Finite vs. Lasting

Experiences built around users and their tasks typically have defined beginning and end points—success can be marked with a definitive stopping point. Brands prefer interactions with lingering effects.

by Kenneth J. Weiss

Experience Forces
Versus IT Forces

Experience Forces

IT Forces

Expected Flows

Producible Flows

Intuition

Familiarity

Balanced UI

Function-First UI

Personally Relevant

Exception Averse

Small UI Difference

Big Production

Build What We Need

Use What We Bought

Never Asked

Never Knew

Toward The Ideal User Experience

This infographic is governed by the Creative Commons
Attribution-Non-Commercial ShareAlike 2.5 License.
creativecommons.org

www.Slightware.com

SOME RIGHTS RESERVED

Experience Forces Vs. IT Forces

User Experience and Information Technology, IT, should be best friends. Should be. But, just as friends sometimes fight, UX and IT are often on opposites sides of the scrum when it comes to dynamics within digital experiences.

Expected Flows vs. Producible Flows

Good user research will show the expected order of events within a flow from the user's perspective. These flows might concern how to apply for a checking account, how to reserve a book at the library, how to download a song, or an almost endless number of other sequential tasks. The developers writing the code for an experience may have a different opinion than the users. When building the library check-out process, for example, a developer might say, "Based upon the current database structure that runs the library web site, people need to create an account before they can add a book to their book bag." This may be completely contrary to the desired flows of the user. The user probably says, "Why would I create an account if there is really nothing I want to reserve." Identifying these discrepancies is an essential part of managing a project. Either additional development re-sources will be needed to create the expected flow, or the user experience will need to be amended to gracefully lead users through an awkward order of events.

Intuition vs. Familiarity

As a user interacts with an experience, they are in part guided by their intuition—their thoughts about what to do. Intuition, however, is not always capable of filling in gaps within the experience, and sometimes these gaps are the product of a developer's familiarity. The developer may omit help text, instructions or labels, because *the developer* knows what to do. These gaps often become evident in usability tests and reviews. A person using a web site or application will get "stuck," and the developer will say helpfully, "Then you just..." The longer a developer has worked on a system, the greater the chances that an intuition/familiarity gap could exist.

Balanced UI (User Interface) vs. Function-First

While the user experience team might strive for a balance between function, aesthetics and usability within an experience, an IT-dominant team may accidentally favor the functions. For example, a UI professional might break a long series of user inputs into multiple screens to create a logical beginning, middle and end to a flow. The developer might offer a solution where user interactions expand or contract the interface to add or remove choices sequestering the experience into one screen which may be flashy, but not necessarily usable.

Small points within the experience might be subject to the same conflict. For example, a UI person might feel that a drop down box needs to be accompanied by a "go" button to initiate the action. The developer may feel that making a drop down selection and simply unclicking the mouse is sufficient to trigger the action – a button would just be clutter. This is a common example of balance working contrary to a function-first mindset.

Personally Relevant vs. Exception Averse

An experience is always more successful when the user feels as though it has been tailored to them. It feels easy when the user needs to spend little or no time filtering out extraneous

100

information. Imagine using the parts guide on a web site to find a replacement coffee pot for a coffeemaker. On one site, the user goes through a series of drop downs and is presented with a page that displays, *"Your replacement pot is A123456."* The second site requires a few less inputs and displays the following, *"Your replacement pot may be A123456 or A123457. Not all pots fit standard units. If using a machine without an automatic timer, use the -7. Check manual for details."* Programming the second web site was easier, because the code did not need to accommodate for all of the exceptions within the data, but the user was faced with a set of results that was less helpful. In order to make an experience personally relevant, the burden of handling exceptions needs to fall on the developers.

Small UI Difference vs. Big Production

Interface designers and UX professionals often look to employ very small differences within the interface to bring about specific results. Accomplished UX pros run complex A/B tests to identify the effects of moving buttons, changing fonts, tweaking colors, etc. These changes may increase the number of items placed in a shopping cart, improve the response rate to an email offer, or move a variety of other critical metrics. Many companies, though, don't have this type of multivariate or A/B test infrastructure in place, and instead rely on best practices, and small purposeful decisions to move the needle. IT team members do not always appreciate the value of what appears to be inconsequential changes.

The conversation sounds comical but is truly painful.

Designer: "Can you make this line of text blue?"

101

Developer: "Blue?"

Designer: "Yes, blue. Here's the hex value."

Developer: "Which blue is not really the issue, because in order to change that we need to (blah, blah, blah)."

Designer: "I just need it to be blue."

Developer: "Does it really matter that much? Really?"

Any innocent bystander at production meetings has heard this conversation dozens of times. The little changes DO matter, but in fairness to the developer, they CAN be a big production.

Build What We Need vs. Use What We Bought

The market creates exciting new user experience possibilities every day. Innovations from companies like Google, Apple and Adobe continually raise the bar for the quality of user experiences. Brands need to evolve their digital experiences to keep pace, and UX professionals are continually challenging themselves to create new ways to present the brand. What happens? UX professionals bring ideas to their development partners that may not be compatible with current infrastructure. IT is left to utter phrases like, "Our in-house media asset management system does not support zoomable images," "The mapping application in our web site does not support door-to-door driving directions," and "We paid the consultants <big number goes here> dollars to develop our library of content templates—can't we use one of those?" Good IT management seeks to maximize the return on investment— get more mileage out of what's been

102

purchased in the past. The realm of user experience, however, is driven by what's going on now, and in the future.

Never Asked vs. Never Knew

Does technology create new opportunities, or does the vision of new user experiences drive technology? Good question. The answer: yes to both. Where does this symbiotic relationship collapse? Communication. Developers can bring a lot to the table. A lot. *If* they are asked to join the table. When developers are pushed to a discrete place in the project order, many of the exciting possibilities are missed. The brand steward and UX professional who treat developers like a production resource probably do not think to ask a lot of questions, and the developer who does not know the overall context of the project doesn't know what to offer.

Setting: The launch party for a new web site.

Developer: "Great job, Mr. UX Guy. Too bad we did not implement the RSS function in the content management system. That would have been cool."

UX Guy: "What? That's built in? I never thought to ask about RSS..."

Developer: "Until I saw the whole thing together, I never knew that it would be useful..."

(Uncomfortable party pause.)

Experience forces and IT forces will be present in every project. UX is not always right. IT is not always right. Neither is always wrong. The forces need to be understood, and both

103

sides need to be mutually valued. UX people can learn a lot from IT, and IT can learn a lot from UX pros.

Experience Forces vs. Business (Corporate) Forces

Digital experiences are subject to corporate forces. That's a reality. No matter how powerful the stakeholder or how respected the development lead, a variety of forces can knock a good experience off track.

Read-with-Ease vs. Legalese

Most brands want to be reader-friendly, but when the subject matter is technical, it gets tricky. When it is healthcare, be careful. When it is financial, watch out. Digital experiences for mortgages, insurance, personal banking, etc., are often saturated with disclaimers, footnotes, and paragraph after paragraph of legalese. While the UX team begs for ease, the legal team mandates complete, accurate and detailed information.

Ah-Ha! vs. CBA

Great users experience delight – they create that magic ah-ha! feeling! But is it possible to plan for both ah-ha and a bullet-proof Cost Benefit Analysis (CBA)? Companies want near-sure things, or at least they want to know what they will get for their money. Creativity and innovation do not fall neatly into CBA's and many organizations do not have dedicated funds for experience innovation. Product innovation? Service innovation? Sure, those functions have budgets, but not experience innovation.

by Kenneth J. Weiss

Experience Forces Versus Business Forces

Experience Forces

Business Forces

Read-With-Ease

Legalese

Ah Ha!

CBA

UXE

SME

Empathetic Reality

Use Do/Hubris

Committed

Committee

Information

Data

50,000 Foot Perspective

Silo Myopia

Toward The Ideal User Experience

This infographic is governed by the Creative Commons Attribution-Non-Commercial ShareAlike 2.5 License. creativecommons.org

SOME RIGHTS RESERVED

www.Slightware.com

UXE vs. SME

User Experience Experts (UXEs) need to welcome Subject Matter Experts (SMEs) to every user experience project. That is not always easy. Often the thunder of "I know this market," "I know this customer," "I know this product," etc., drowns out the nuances of a carefully crafted user experience strategy.

Companies typically do not put the manager of customer service in charge of legal issues, but will roll the dice and put a marketing or IT person in charge of digital experiences. These people may be great at their jobs, but UX is a DIFFERENT job.

Empathetic Reality vs. Use/Do Hubris

Sometimes project stakeholders make the mistake of assuming that users will interact with a system in the same way they would. "Hmm, that's not how I'd use <insert experience here>." "That's not what I do when I'm online."

What is needed is a true understanding of the user's reality. If a computer application may have older users, please, make the type bigger or at least adjustable. If a web site might be used on a portable device, make sure the links can be selected without accidentally triggering other functions.

Use/Do Hubris is wicked and often goes to the ball with its ugly cousins: "Well, I like THAT color," and "THAT picture doesn't look good to me."

Committed vs. Committee

A good project has shared and understood objectives—the execution, however, may be a bit more subjective. No

106

amount of due process can deny the fact that many parts of a user experience design rely heavily on creativity and artistic vision. Good UX pros bring passion to every project – they are committed. Nothing, however, ruins an experience like too many opinions – the dreaded committee. Team members, stakeholders and clients love to participate in the creative process; for them it is a welcome break from the more tedious parts of the project. But just because they CAN pick colors and fonts does not mean they SHOULD. Any good digital experience needs creative guidance from standards documentation and a qualified art director. Others may have opinions, but the art director or designer should have the final say.

Information vs. Data

Data about a user experience must not be mistaken for information about a user experience. Often, reporting will show what happened, but it will not be married with the details of what might have changed within the user experience. History has shown that very small changes in interfaces can create large changes in user behavior. If the fact that a change had taken place was not adequately noted in a report, some other variable may get the credit, or blame, for the difference in the data. A good analyst must be able to credibly work with data and understand the evolution of the experience.

50,000 Foot Perspective vs. Silo Myopia

Many digital experiences are driven by the business objectives of departments or constituencies within an organization: advertising wants to communicate the brand, customer service wants to reduce calls, etc. Digital experiences however, even very focused ones, often draw upon multiple

107

areas of the company, and the experience needs to retain that bigger perspective. For example, almost every part of the company wants a piece of the home page. Have a recruiting problem? Make the "jobs" link bigger on the home page. Great new product to introduce? Put it on the home page. Complete a major acquisition? How about a news ticker on the home page. Great new hire? How about a pic on the home page?

Less conspicuous digital experiences like an online account log-in page may also be the target for messaging by different groups within the company. "Customers should know that a rebate is available," "We should let customers know a great new color was introduced," "We've just opened up a service center near them" and on and on. While each of these may have merit, there are lots of messages competing for space.

Each stakeholder has some degree of myopia about what MAY be included within an experience. A good user experience person is the arbiter of such requests, understands how to balance them within the larger perspective, and above all else, knows when to edit.

The Cause Network of Slightware

When the internet was originally conceived back in the 1960s it was built around a decentralized model which insured that killing off one part of the system would not neutralize the entire system. Irony. Irony. Today's brands are subject to a vast network of forces that cause slightware. Killing one force? Again, it still will not kill the network.

The Forces of Business Operations

The drive to do business faster, smarter and more profitably inevitably leads to reliance on automated processes and operational environments that are not brand-friendly.

Outsourcing

Despite all of the potential economic benefits of outsourcing, it always proves to be challenge to the long-term health of a brand. Outsourcing requires knowledge transfer. Basic product and process knowledge comes first; brand strategy, at best, is a distant second.

Warehousing and distribution are perennial front runners for outsourcing. Companies see themselves as builders of brands – not warehouses. So inventory management systems are put in place. Call centers are established. Extranets are built. Each is designed to help answer the simplest of questions: "Where is it?" "When will I have it?" "How many do you have?" This outsourced solution is intended to run in the background. At its best, it is imperceptible to the customer. In reality, the best case scenario is not always achieved. These questions can be met with disjointed phone calls, emails that don't quite match the reality, and one-way communication that strives just to get an answer. Not communications that build brands.

Other outsourced activities are much closer to the customer. Service and support, warranty registration, and many others are all directly connected to the brand in the customer's mind. Customers regularly call help desks…and hold…and hold…and hold. Other phone calls are met with a labyrinth of prompts. Sometimes the hold message pushes the customer to a web site. When a human finally does answer, that person is often, literally and figuratively, a thousand miles away from the minds that crafted the product and the brand. A customer calling in for a warranty claim is often made responsible for documenting the entire evolution of the sales process. "Don't you already know all this?" thinks the customer.

Offshoring

Offshoring has many of the challenges of outsourcing with the additional challenges of distance and culture. Many people have called 800 numbers only to experience sound quality that mirrors old Apollo mission tapes. The static, clicks, buzzes and beeps are signals that the experience is not smooth, not immediate and not personal. The customer service rep seems, and may in fact be, on the other side of the planet.

Some offshore customer service firms have attempted to augment their knowledge systems with cultural training. Reps are trained in how to deliver scripts and phrases with an American accent. In some instances the reps create robust character profiles: "I am 24. I grew up in the Midwest. I love college football. I like snow and rain. I have a dog. He is a Husky named King." All of these tactics, and more, are designed to make the rep seem more pleasing and create a better brand experience.

Automation and Self Service

The march toward the automation of self service began years ago with optical systems. People attempting a wide variety of tasks were given worksheets with questions or choices, and the answers were segmented with small circles

110

called bubbles. The user simply filled in the bubbles to mark their choices. (Many state lottery systems still use the same technology to allow people to pick their winning digits.) OCR eventually matured to OCR, Optical Character Recognition. This allowed people to complete items like health-care forms while carefully writing words by breaking out the letters into individual boxes. The forms would then be scanned and the technology would recognize the letterforms and store everything as usable data. The downside of both of these systems was that companies still had to move and store paper.

The next evolution was self service IVR, Interactive Voice Response. These systems allowed people to call telephone numbers and make selections using the phone keypad. A typical scenario could include a person receiving a work-sheet in the mail, making a series of choices, and then using the phone to key in their selections. This was considered "better" since paper only had to move in one direction and the onus of inputting the data was placed on the user.

The web came along and provided a huge boost to the self service movement. Now people can be made to do EVERYTHING. Apply for a mortgage. Get a car insurance quote. Trade stocks. Sign up for health insurance benefits. Change a home address for human resources. Register for college classes. And on and on. Costs were absolutely, posi-tively squeezed out of the systems.

So what's wrong with automation and self service? This is: The brand is rarely incorporated as it should be, and the user always has the nagging question, "Did I just do that right since nobody helped me?"

111

Downsizing, Forced Retirements and Layoffs from Mergers

Downsizing, retirements and layoffs all mean that people are leaving a company. On some occasions, companies have either extra capacity or redundant human capital. In most cases, however, the "getting smaller and getting smarter" thinking means that systems are expected to handle more of the burden of day-to-day operations. However, people can assimilate brand strategy much more readily than systems. People are also capable of having great passion for a brand. People also know customers. People also know the nuances of buying and owning a product. People...are vitally important to brands.

The Forces of the Information Economy

In the end, the Information Economy will be great for brands...some brands, anyway...but the end is far, far away. The space between now and then is strewn with potential problems.

Disintermediation

Disintermediation is a fancy term for "cutting out the middle man." On the surface, this should help consumers and brands. A layer between the customer and the brand owner is removed. Communication should be more direct, and costs are squeezed out of the system. What is often overlooked if the fact that "middle men" have spent years, if not decades, understanding and satisfying the needs of customers. The middle men, those in the distribution channel, created vast pools of product knowledge, customer insight and

112

market intelligence. All of this is important to brands and brand satisfaction.

Market Transparency

Ten years ago when our fathers went shopping for snow tires, they checked the newspaper, chatted with the neighbors, made a few calls and visited a handful of places in town. That's what they had to work with. That's how they answered the questions of "Who carries what?" and "How much does that cost?" Businesses and brands had ample opportunities to use physical distance and a dearth of available information to keep people in the dim, if not in the dark. Now consumers can easily research products, find alternatives, locate retailers and compare prices. The idea of scarcity in the marketplace has been replaced with the challenge of almost infinite choice. Many web sites and digital experiences have made the idea of comparison shopping their focal point.

Niche Market Viability

In the past, catalogs, direct mail, magazine advertising, direct response television and phone solicitation were considered the best ways to tap niche markets.

Each offered some great advantages:

Catalogs married to 800 numbers offered scalable, illustrative vehicles for displaying a wide range of products while allowing for immediate ordering. The mailing lists could also be incredibly well targeted.

Direct mail, like catalogs, could be driven by incredibly sophisticated targeting models for address selection. The relatively low

113

production costs allowed for fast and economic testing of creative executions and offers.

Magazines provided narrow, well-defined target audiences, reasonable rates for space, and the flexibility of different sized advertisements.

Direct response television (DRTV) allowed for large reach, the flexibility of 15-, 30-, 60- or 120-second formats. Long-form DRTV included 30-minute and 60-minute shows that were sometimes run consecutively a.k.a. "the infomercial." DRTV offered the excitement of demonstrations, a passionate host, repeated calls-to-action and the ability to target people night and day for optimum use of media dollars.

Phone solicitation was a wonderful industry prior to the Do Not Call registry. Well-trained phone reps with back pockets full of carefully crafted counter-objections could sell, sell, sell. Luckily for dinner time, phone solicitation has been dramatically reduced mainly to use by charities and political endeavors.

Although the tactics discussed above were referred to in the past tense, they still remain viable. Even a true believer in the digital ways of the web would agree that they can be effective, and will continue to be effective for some time.

The web and digital technologies have allowed marketers to effectively go after very small but lucrative markets. Web sites can be constructed with brands, messaging and products to appeal to very specific people. No longer must a company put out a single "Dog Lovers" catalog. They can have separate web sites for schnauzers, poodles, and even shnoodles. Yes, shnoodles.

The ability to economically create various front ends for store systems has been supercharged by paid search market-

114

ing. Now brands can hyper target users looking for infi-
nitely specific things like a "comfortable leather collar with
buckle for collies."

These niche marketing opportunities allow brands to be
incredibly relevant to people, but also offer a disastrously
tempting, low-cost opportunity to shove a brand into a
space where it does not belong.

The Global Economy

The World Wide Web is not always completely worldly. The
web that each person experiences, especially in the US, is
actually regional in intentional and unintentional ways. Not
every site offers multilingual capabilities. A person can find
their favorite brands web site for any country, but they
might not be able to read and understand the language to
get a feel for the promise and presentation of the brand.
Search engines *can* see content all across the world but tend
to only show users content based upon language, IP address
and country-level domain. For instance a person in the US
searching with German search terms is still more likely to
see listings for ".com" web sites rather than ".de" web sites.
(".de" is the country code for Germany.)

In other respects, the web lives up to its global promise.
Users can easily read web sites intended for English audiences from places like Ireland, Australia and England.
Companies wanting to project their brands into a foreign
marketplace can easily do so. News services provide native
language stories for expatriates around the globe. Global
industries that are better defined by business practices and
markets rather than tenuous geopolitical boundaries can
easily stay connected.

115

This balance of what is possible and what is practical for brands on a global level requires insight and experience. Showing a happy family driving down the highway on a web site? Are they driving, or are they "motoring?" On which side of the car is the steering wheel? On which side of the road are they traveling? What happens when users in different markets are being charged different prices? Online currency converters quickly allow people to do the math and gain a new perspective on the brand. What happens when a web site feels interminably slow because the data is flowing across a transoceanic cable rather than being served locally? Brands looking to be "global" need to be smart and culturally sensitive.

Mass Customization

The maturation of the web along with the remarkable improvements in manufacturing technologies and theories have provided users with the opportunity to order customized products online. Consumers can go to art sites to pick images, frames and mats. Consumers can use configurators at automotive web sites to build cars with the perfect combination of style, performance and accessories. Consumers can tailor their mortgages online. Consumers can even have a pair of jeans made to fit their body perfectly. Customization is an appealing prospect, but the standards for execution are quite high. What happens if a person buys a framed Monet print online, but the green of the mat board doesn't quite match the green they saw on the computer monitor? What's the return policy? Who pays for return shipping? Can the consumer change their mind completely and get their money back? And, what ultimately happens to the returned item? Won't the promise of the brand be damaged

116

if consumers find a web site that sells all of the stuff that people send back? If the cost of destroying or reworking the product needs to be added into the overall costs structure, will the online price advantage be harmed?

Lots of opportunities—lots of challenges.

Low Cost Computing

Does technology support business models or does technology become business models? It's an interesting question that is made more interesting when technology gets obscenely cheap. Today, servers, storage, bandwidth and licenses for applications cost a fraction of what they did only a few years ago. Business and marketing plans that needed to be airtight a few years ago because of the massive capital investment required to get digital companies off the ground are a little more fuzzy now. In some instances, hungry programmers start building "things" and the business model "evolves." Many of these startups are funded from personal checking accounts and credit cards. This is great for the industry in general. Lots of new choices and experiences for consumers. Lots of new ideas. Lots of outlets for technological breakthroughs. This is not always great for brands. The brand is sometime relegated to "logo" status in the UI. Companies quickly come and go. The fabled internet dead pool has a few more floating corpses. Even existing companies get a little less rigorous in attempting pilots, tests and experiments because the financial pain of failure has been lessened.

The Amazon-Google-Yahoo-eBay Bar

Do you want to make an e-commerce guy at a mid-sized company miserable? Point out all of the great features that

117

Amazon-Google-Yahoo-eBay have added. Then say, "We should do that, too!" Better yet, enthusiastically say it in front of the CEO and mug for affirmation. These sites set the bar really high and both consumers and bosses expect brands to follow. Their new features make their brands look good. The delta between those sites and other sites makes the also-ran brands look bad. Many small business advocates celebrated the fact that the web created a level playing field. Guess what? It's a level playing field, and the digital experiences of all types of brands will be judged against each other—especially those who nudge the bar ever higher each day.

Information and Experience as Product

Great digital experiences are worth paying for. On the web, these can be subscription-based sites for games or information and can also include online/offline combinations such as delivery-to-home services for groceries or movies. The world of mobile includes dozens of examples in the form of text messaging, picture messaging, games, ring tones, and other services— information or experiences that are sold as discrete products or at least add-ons.

These spaces are competitive, and the arms race for more features and revenues must be managed carefully. User adoption and satisfaction is paramount. In the early days of the web, internet service providers had to manage their churn. This was the measure of the number of new customers in for the number of customers out. Churn was caused by better offers from competitors, lack of use or the inability to understand how to use the service.

For information and experiences as products to succeed, the

possibilities can not outpace simplicity and usability. Too often information services or experience-based subscriptions are so incredibly over-complicated that mass adoption is not likely to occur.

Free and Premium Service Models

The great scalability of web technologies has given rise to multi-tiered usage models. The typical format is to give a little of the site or service for free, and then charge users for a premium version once they are hooked. Dating sites, music services, financial sites, news sites and others successfully use this model. The structure raises some interesting implications for brands. Giving something away for free should induce trial, but can lead to a cheapening of the brand's perceived value. Transitioning a user to the paid service may feel confrontational, or the walled components may leave the user feeling that the brand is holding back. As similar competitive services slide the free/paid line in either direction, users re-evaluate their perception of the brand. "Hey, that other service gives me twice as much photo storage for photos for the same price." "Wait a minute! That other service offers unlimited storage for FREE!"

Function for Eyeballs Models

Services that offer unlimited anything are typically trading functionality for eyeballs. They are aggregating audiences that can be sold to advertisers. "Eyeballs" is a slightly outdated concept referring to the fact that a web site or experience had an audience of people who could "see" ads. Now whenever audiences are collected, so is a vast amount of demographic, psychographic and usage data. Even the most cynical users might be surprised by exactly how much information can be collected.

119

Sociocultural Forces

Society continues to change. Brand strategy and brand management need to prepare for the realities of a changing workforce and marketplace.

Job Transience

Today's college graduates will have more then 5 different jobs in their field and a large number will completely change industries at least once before they retire. Companies need to plan for training and knowledge transfer. "Fresh thinking" can be good, but a company's revolving front door means that some very profound understanding of brands can leave at almost any moment. This requires a strategy of embedding knowledge within systems rather than people.

Migration to the US

The melting pot of America is as hot as ever. Even in the post 9/11 world, the flow of all types of people continues, albeit hindered by bureaucracy. Smart, bright people are coming to the US bringing their own cultures and ideas. Often they rise to influential marketing and IT positions.

Gen Y Workforce

Volumes have been written on this demographic segment. Suffice to say, they are good at using technology. They are in touch with cultural trends, and they can be downright stubborn about how they think things should be done.

Boomer Bubble

The rise of Gen Y is coming along as millions of Boomers will be retiring. Their perspectives, attitudes and appreciations are sometimes miles apart.

The archetypical conversation goes something like this:

"Before I retire, I'd like to tell you some things about the brand."

"I know all about the brand."

"You do? How?"

"Google, YouTube, Facebook."

"Oh. Well, let me tell you how consumers have been using some of the features of our latest product."

"Not necessary. We will be changing all of those to be web-enabled."

Hmmm. Good for brands? Bad for brands? Probably lots of both.

Diversity in the Workplace

Diversity in the workplace generally refers to ethnic and religious diversity along with differences in sexual orientation. This concept will grow to include dramatic differences in age, work schedules, educational backgrounds, abilities, disabilities and more. In short, the workplace will reflect society in general. How can such a wide spectrum of people be aligned behind brands that are supposed to remain focused and resolute?

121

Knowledge Workers

One of the interesting effects of the manufacturing boom of World War II was the growth of personal power tools. Workers used new types of tools on the job, and wanted them at home. This same thing is happening with today's knowledge workers. Where our grandfathers would tinker in the garage, people today are tinkering on their computers retouching photos, reviewing family finances, running small online businesses and more. Rather than just using consumer-grade applications they are investing in more powerful computers and software.

Gaming

Music, film and TV have welcomed games as the fourth pillar of the entertainment industry. Brands need to know how to react. The 30-second prime time commercial is no longer the go-to mechanism for building brands that it once was. Teens, tweens and twenty-somethings have been spending more time with games.

Computer and Device Literacy

Everyone is getting better using technology. Yes, there are "old school" holdouts: no cell phone, no ATM card, no internet connection, but for the most part, consumers of all types are getting more adept with computers, cell phones and digital experiences including self-service checkouts and kiosks in businesses.

Time Compression

The pace of change and the expectations of what can be accomplished during any given period of time continues to accelerate. This notion of "time compression" was coined by

Agnieszka Winkler in the '90s. (Wow, even that sounds like a long time ago.) Fashions and fad change more quickly. Musical artists leap from social web sites to the Billboard charts. Bad news travels faster. Reality shows turn average people into celebrities. The series finale turns most of them back. Can brands still have lasting power?

Technology Evolution and Skill Set Obsolescence

Technology is continuing to advance at an incredible pace powered by remarkable breakthroughs in programming languages and processing power. Is it possible for the average Jane or Joe to stay up to date on all of the possibilities when confronted with the challenges of the daily grind? Do younger people who have always lived with ever-changing technology have an advantage in learning new technologies? The answers are "maybe" and "definitely." The challenge for companies and brands will be to keep older, brand-informed employees up to speed while making sure that leading edge employees understand larger strategic brand initiatives when using tactical technologies.

Technology Forces within Companies

Technology lets employees do more. And, more of that more is about the brand. Touch the brand more. Contribute to the brand more. Shape the brand more. Deliver the brand more.

Don't let the alphabet soup deter you. Understanding the software landscape is essential.

DTP (Desktop Publishing) Becomes Digital Marketing Production

Twenty years ago brand professionals worried about the first generation of desktop publishing. Corporate brochures, product sell sheets and other basic documentation could be done by almost anyone. Today, sales presentations, photo galleries, web sites, and even videos have joined the roster of DIY marketing possibilities. Is this really great for companies or really bad for brands?

CIM (Customer Interaction Management) /CCM (Customer Contact Management) /CRM (Customer Relationship Management)

The driving idea behind these technologies is simple: A company should have a single view of its dialogue with a customer, an understanding of the nature of the dialogue and knowledge of a customer's purchase history. When executed correctly these technologies help reduce costs and improve revenues while producing a better customer experience. What a great win-win-win! If done incorrectly or incompletely the gaps can be very damaging. A person might pay a bill online and call customer service with another question, only to have the rep remind them to pay their bill. An enthusiastic salesperson calls an account to pitch a new product only to find out that the account still has hard feelings about some previous products that the account has discussed "repeatedly" with another person. The company which is trying to "work smart" ends up "looking stupid."

124

CMS (Content Management Systems)

Content management systems are intended to separate the chores of maintaining content from those of maintaining a web site. By using a system of templates, publishing rules and workflows, those people who know the content can manage the site without knowing the intricacies of web site code and servers. In order for a content management system to work effectively, the page templates and navigational structures need to be pre-built with a rock solid understanding of the users, likely tasks and the content itself. Although the templates are not inherently fixed, companies often make the mistake of ignoring the need for ongoing updates and the continual investment in new templates. After all, users' tasks and needs change, and the site should as well. As a result, new pieces of content are shoehorned into templates, new content relationships are not configured within the system, and navigation is not updated to reflect new structures. The system, although technically operational, would be broken and the brand would be damaged.

DAM (Digital Asset Management)

One of the realities that comes with the increased ability to create photos, diagrams, copy, video, etc., is the need to manage the assets throughout the enterprise. Who has used what picture? Where? If legal decides that a certain product usage shot opens the company to potential litigation, how quickly can all of the instances of such use be identified? If the past use of a licensed stock photo was questioned, can the usage history be identified? If a product's packaging has been updated, which sales people are using a glamour shot of the product in presentations?

Great digital asset management is an essential tool for brand control and protection.

RFID (Radio Frequency Identification Tags)

RFID sensors are small chips placed on products that provide a signal to shipping and warehousing systems. Companies can actually see products flow through the supply and demand chains to optimize inventory levels and better understand demand cycles. Keeping a very tight control on inventory can produce massive savings for companies.

The technology will ultimately need to be married with predictive models. What happens if, out of the blue, Oprah mentions a product on her show? A razor-thin inventory model will probably not be able to accommodate the surge at the retail level. How can those types of events be predicted? Will brands have to live with the potential disappointment of products being sold out?

IT at the Table

Senior information technology executives within companies are now being looked upon as part of the strategic team rather than just people who help execute plans. This is great news for technology and brands provided that IT executives are aware of the pains of slightware.

Technology Forces at the Consumer Level

Technology has changed consumers from passive receptors of brands into active contributors to the brand dialogue. Technology at the consumer level is scary good, and getting

Kenneth J. Weiss

better every day which can be a scary bad thing that keeps getting scarier for brands.

DRM - Digital Rights Management

Does "I can download it" mean "It is free?" No. Absolutely not. But many consumers act that way. So companies have created ways to manage downloads referred to as Digital Rights Management (DRM). The downloads might expire. They might run on only certain types of devices. If the user does not obey the usage terms they might get sued. DRM has been applied to music, TV shows, movies and books.

Despite the numerous transgressions companies continue to experiment with more lenient systems including rights-free arrangements where the download can be purchased once and duplicated, moved from device to device and even shared.

The consumer acceptance of DRM is gradually fading away. A brand that is attempting to protect itself might be viewed as old, outdated and downright selfish.

PDCM – (Personal Digital Content Management/Manipulation)

How many records were in a great music collection a few years ago? How many photo albums were owned by the average family? How many movies were on the shelf in the family room? Today people are owners and creators of content. Lots of content. Thousands of pictures. Thousands of songs. The tools to capture and edit content, PCDM tools, are easy to use and provide great quality. Unlike the early days of the web where "everyone could publish" if they knew some basic programming or had the patience to suffer

127

through cumbersome widgets, people today can easily create and disseminate content on the web and on mobile devices.

Wireless, Broadband and Internet 2

Internet access will soon be everywhere, and it is getting faster – amazingly faster. It is also getting cheaper, if not completely free. A digital divide may always exist to some degree between those who have access to digital infrastructure (home computers and internet access) and those who don't, but the world and the millions and millions of target audiences therein will be more connected. This connectivity will be defined by greater speeds, connectivity while on the go and greatly reduced costs. A brand's story and a wealth of contextual information will be instantaneously available.

Chapter Five

Beating Slightware – How To, Why To and Who To

Slightware is not going anywhere. The key question for business is to decide how to set a course that will overtake this speeding bullet. The solution will be a bit different for each organization, but, similar to other business challenges, problem diagnosis, people with specific skills, process definition and proven systems are essential. If this sounds like a tall order, just start with a little UX common sense.

The Traditional E's of Usability

Usability is a term commonly employed to describe how easily a person can achieve a successful outcome within an experience. It should be a goal of every company for every experience, but it can be elusive.

Both offline and online experiences can be analyzed for their usability. Instruction manuals, paper forms, user guides, and packaging can all be evaluated. The physicality of these objects makes their level of usability easier to discern (but not completely easy) for the typical business person. Digital experiences – the user experiences of the slightware world – are more difficult to gauge.

Usability takes restraint and knowledge. Unfortunately many companies pursue usability with the "I'll know it when I see it" strategy. What's the problem with that? The "I." Usability needs to be determined from the user's perspective. Just because the business sponsor or developer

129

thinks something works doesn't mean the user will actually find it usable. The five traditional, time-tested E's of usability provide a framework for understanding the usability of experiences: Effective, Efficient, Engaging, Error Aware and Easy to Learn.

Effective

Effectiveness is a measure of the completeness and accuracy of the outcomes of an experience. Simple questions help frame the judgment: Was the user able to complete the task? Were all of the outcomes accurate? For instance, a person could successfully book an airline ticket online but if they went to Aukland rather than Oakland, the experience would be neither effective nor accurate.

Practiced user experience professionals understand how to group tasks, provide inline help functions, trigger prompts, create meaningful instructions, determine appropriate labels and make other similar decisions to help a user achieve complete and accurate outcomes.

Efficient

Efficiency is a measure of speed to an outcome. The top line metric is time-on-task. Other metrics can include the number of clicks, thumbstrokes, screens, etc.

For a typical web application such as an online checkout or registration, the layout of forms, the flow between pages, tabbing between form fields and the use of devices like drop downs, radio buttons and check boxes all play a part in efficiency. A good understanding of the target user along with any relevant assumptions and preconditions is absolutely essential.

130

Beware! It is not always desirable to chip away at efficiency metrics. "Shorter! Fewer!" people demand. Even so, completeness and accuracy should not be sacrificed. Nor should certainty or user confidence. Online applications such as bill paying and banking are better served with a few extra clicks that will make the user feel substantially more confident and on-track.

Engaging

Some tasks are not optional for users. A person will make themselves struggle through online experiences such as paying a parking ticket, registering for a class, or buying a hard-to-find item. When a task is not necessary, or a workaround feels possible, users can be fickle. If the search function on a website does not work? Forget it, surfing might work. Having trouble downloading a ring tone? Perhaps one of the defaults will suffice.

An experience needs to be engaging enough to capture the user's attention. A certain "ah-ha" factor needs to be present. The unskilled user experience professional or mis-assigned business person often brings a heavy hand to the experience with the modern day equivalents of spinning logos – or worse yet – flaming logos. The user can be engaged by the style of the graphics, the feel of the interaction, the clarity of the information presentation, the use of rich media elements and more, but it's a thin line between engagement and distraction.

Error Aware

Users will make mistakes within a system. Not only do new users make mistakes, but experienced users with extended time between uses will also make mistakes. Accessing an

131

experience from a web browser on one occasion and a mobile device on the next can cause errors as well. Even if all is going well, an unclear instruction line, a sticky mouse and hundreds of other factors can lead to errors.

The best designers of experiences are aware of this certainty and prepare for it. The first line of defense is error prevention. Smart, little choices in the construction of the interface and interaction help prevent errors. For instance, if the experience will require phone numbers in discrete segments, a good interface will break out the area code, exchange and latter digits into three fields rather than relying on the user to include spaces or dashes. Imagine the user who is faced with the instruction on an auction site, "Provide an opening amount for your bid." Should they include the dollar sign or not? What little finishing touch could prevent the error?

The second component is error recovery. This is the experience's ability to bail the user out of the "oh, crap" moments. Usable systems provide well-thought-out ways for the user to recover.

An "undo" button in a design application is an obvious form of error recovery. Not every system works that well. Many websites fail to integrate the on-screen navigation with the back button. If the user chooses the right one, they can correct their mistake. The wrong one will fire an error message. But which one is the right one? Hmmm. Since errors are inevitable, great consideration should be given to error recovery.

Easy to Learn

Whether a device is used just one time or once every day, it needs to be easy to use. Some user experiences demand a

132

very low learning curve. ATM machines, airline kiosks, digital photo output centers in grocery stores, and other devices are referred to as "walk up and use devices." These can have little or no learning curve. Other user experience and devices may take some level of commitment. Too difficult to learn? The user may give up or not completely explore the features. Too easy? Enough value may not be delivered.

Being easy to learn extends across visits or instances of use. During the second or third use, the user might have slightly different tasks, need to expand a task or they may need to build upon a previous accomplishment.

Avoiding the Creeps

A project might start with a great vision, solid objectives, tight requirements and a good development team, but things can eventually stray. What starts as a small concession to a request opens the door to other slight deviations from the plan. These are not changes, but simple small ways where the project begins to creep.

Look out. Things can get creepy.

Creeping Featurism, a.k.a. Feature Creep

This is the B-movie classic of the creeps. Creeping featurism is that nasty tendency of the development team or key stakeholder to add another feature, the dreaded "one more thing." Why? Sometimes this is a feeble attempt to provide a last minute point of differentiation, satisfy a tiny market segment, or to try to pull out of a project nose dive. Unfortunately, in most cases, it happens just because it can, and nobody thinks to stop it. The phrase "While we are at it..."

133

should bring looks of revulsion rather than curiosity and consideration.

Simplicity is killed by this creep. An experience that the user could have quickly and comfortably learned turns into an exercise of deciphering what to ignore. The once-in-a-blue-moon features compete with the everyday features for the time and attention of the user. They gobble up interface real estate, create unnecessary troubleshooting problems, make the user manual more cumbersome, increase time-to-learn and on, and on, and on.

Uncle Al Einstein said it best, ""Make everything as simple as possible, but not simpler."

Creeping Elegance

Sounds charming in a Stepford way, doesn't it? Creeping elegance is the over-polishing of the interface. This may be excessive manipulation of the graphics or an over-engineering of behavior.

Even something as simple as a button can suffer from creeping elegance. It can be made too shiny with an overdone shape. The feedback might include an obnoxious sound effect, color change or animation. It might be so polished that it is no longer perceived as a button.

Why is creeping elegance a bad idea? Well, unless the goal is to get mindless giggles through endless eye candy, creeping elegance is an unnecessary distraction to the user. Never has a person said, "Boy, the search engine on that web site did not give me anything useful, but the look of that button when I clicked 'go' – wow!"

134

Einstein rip-off for the day: "Make user experiences beautifully on brand, but no more beautiful."

Creeping Approvers

The approval process should be simple. Ask who has final approval for project elements, document the approvers, and ask them when the time comes.

It is rarely that simple.

Almost any person familiar with the creation of user experiences and software has heard this conversation:

"So what do you think of the UI design?"

"Love it!"

"Great! So it's approved?"

"Absolutely. Love it. Approved."

"Fantastic. We'll get started on the development?"

"Okay. Can I keep this copy? There are a few people I need to show."

Uh-oh. Get ready for death by committee. Creeping approval can happen at all stages of a project, on all parts of a project.

Creeping Input

Getting input is absolutely essential for projects, and invaluable input can be garnered from all corners of the company. Subject matter experts may be the company's C-listers or the people in the call centers.

135

So how does input start to creep?

Input Dominators – Committees, focus groups, and input sessions may be dominated by a person who believes that their input is more meaningful and important than others. This person may even follow up with additional phone calls and emails.

Input Relevancy – When a project gets on a roll, the input may keep on coming and coming. One more call. One more email. Due diligence turns into tangential meandering.

Input After The Fact – Whenever a project's discovery-gathering phase is done - it's done. But…sometimes the exercise of executing the project makes the team more insightful. The temptation to backtrack and ask some clarifying questions can get very alluring.

Creeping Code

Creeping code is also known as software bloat. Software bloat may cross into the areas of creeping elegance and creeping featurism, but usually involves a user experience or software application using large amounts of system resources without any appreciable benefits to the user. Creeping code can intrude on storage, processing power, bandwidth and RAM.

Creeping Deadlines

Deadlines can creep in either direction. In simple projects this may be easy to overcome, but complex projects may require a careful coordination of resources for integration, testing and deployment.

Deadlines can also creep forward. "We have a trade show," "I'm getting pressure from above," "XYZ Corp. can NOT beat us to market," are all signs that the deadline will a get a little creepy.

Creeping Requirements

Remember – anything CAN be done. Smart, innovative discovery can identify many possible tacks for a project. Gut checks, market research and cost-benefit analysis help determine what SHOULD be done. When some form of control beyond limited opinions is not in place, requirements can creep to an area of diminishing returns.

Creeping Data Collection

When a user experience or application is deployed, capturing metrics about its usage it essential. For traditional web sites data points such as page view length, most downloaded files and top entry points are typical. Applications may be measured by total number of functions performed, amount of data processed, length of user sessions and even usage by different audience segments. Aggressive companies and project sponsors may attempt to capture data for all aspects of the experience. The true data needs will creep. Additional code, storage and tools may be needed. At some point, the company may be swimming in a sea of data without any real information.

Creeping Legalism

Legal input is essential for almost all digital experiences. Transactional web sites need disclaimers. Web promotions require rules. Even basic sites need terms and conditions. The legal department may even be called upon to review headlines and copy. The risk and potential costs associated

137

with getting it wrong can be enormous. Good legal professionals are consultative and measured in their requests for changes, but their aversion to risk often leads to a creeping litany of changes that hamper the user experience and brand delivery.

Creeping Verbalism

This little creep is a cousin of creeping legalism, and is the product of well-intentioned but ill-informed stakeholders who find it difficult to refrain from adding one more bullet point, "power-word," or brand reference. Headlines, instructions, labels and other copy elements become swollen and unwieldy – even as the stakeholders think they are adding clarity and specificity.

Creeping Context

Creeping context is most likely to affect projects with longer timeframes and greater complexity. As the project stretches, the original context including the business case, market dynamics, internal climate (both political and technical) and user preferences may shift. This can be gradual, a creep, or abrupt. In extreme cases, obsolescence sets in the day after the launch party.

The Skills Needed To Beat Slightware

Who builds and delivers great digital experiences? Certainly not your dad's marketing department. Sorry, advertising agencies, not you either. Graphic designers, no. Video producers, uh-uh. Programmers, sit back down. The good news is that all of these talented people can play a part in the creation of great digital experiences, but a new distinct set of skills is needed. Here they are (alphabetized for your convenience.)

Brand Strategy

Brand building in the age of slightware starts with proven brand strategy, the traditional thinking around brand management which includes all of the elements of a well-conceived and implemented brand. That's the easy part (although many people never get beyond the brand as veneer rather than as an integral part of every function within a company, but that is some other guy's book). New brand strategy is the ability to conceptualize elements within user experiences designed to build the brand with interaction and an understanding of how the exchange of information creates brand value. This new form of brand strategy requires thinking about system behavior, user preparedness and experience adaptation over short and long periods of time. These dynamics may include a vast number of people or a single individual.

An updated brand acumen also must included the ability to evaluate all types of experiences: web pages, phone scripts, messages generated by dynamic logic, interactions governed by complex rules systems and more.

Content Strategy and Development

What popped to mind when the word "content" traveled 'cross the cerebellum? "Copy"? Ouch! Content includes text, certainly, but also includes audio, video, interactions, testimonials, comments, ratings, user contributed images, and more. Content strategy is the ability to determine how content can be leveraged to create user value within the experience and a greater competitive advantage for the brand.

139

Don't just think about computer screens, either. Mobile devices, music players, game platforms, in-car systems and public kiosks are all venues where content will be consumed and created.

An understanding of content brings new questions. How are all of these types of content created? What's the difference between fluff elements and real, valuable nuggets? How is brand voice balanced with the clarity needed by users? In addition to these issues, content needs to be nailed for completeness, accuracy and all legal considerations. Experienced content strategists and producers need to understand a wide variety of production processes, device considerations, file types, copyright formats, rights-management issues and ongoing management strategies.

Online Campaign Strategy

Ad men of the world, pack your bags! The new campaigns are conversations, and these are inextricably part of the new world of user experience - not the old world of advertising. Today's online strategy requires a thorough understanding of digital systems, test design, analytics, behavioral modeling, production technologies and user systems limitations. The traditional ability to conceptualize campaign frameworks and direct appropriate resources is still necessary but is only part of the answer.

Online Creative Strategy

Back in the recent old days (when people walked uphill both ways to school in the rain, because global warming had eliminated snow) advertising could bank on the power of interruption. TV commercials had to be endured rather than zapped with the DVR, radio came from towers with commercials and not by satellite, and telemarketers could disturb your dinner. Now consumers have a greater choice when it comes to interacting with campaigns. Creative strategy needs to be bigger than "the big idea" and includes an understanding of how to create DESIRED interactions, the optimization of campaigns and the understanding of the technical limitations of digital delivery systems.

Device Knowledge

Things were tough enough for the average digital professional when they had to keep track of a few different browser types (e.g., Netscape v. Microsoft Browser Wars)*, Flash versions and monitor settings. Make a site work on a Mac, add a low- and a high-bandwidth version, and the deed was pretty much done. Messy as that was, it presented a knowable set of variables. Well...things have changed. New browsers are popping up *and* getting market share. Laptops are coming with wider and wider screens while at the same time more hand-held devices are offering really small screens. Browser plug-ins and tool bars are providing different features, and security software is blocking and allowing who knows what. Add to that new hardware and software options for texting, email, picture sharing and media consumption. The possible universe of user experiences gets pretty darn big.

* A more complete trip in the "Wayback Machine" would include monitors with limited colors, a gaggle of AOL browsers and even devices like WebTV.

Digital Systems Knowledge

In the '90s the code found within web pages was both incredible and incredibly simplistic. Incredible because it

141

brought remarkable new opportunities, and simplistic because browsers were only capable of rendering pages with a limited amount of complexity. Today and into the coming years, the realm of web and digital systems will continue to explode. Experiences will get wider—crossing more platforms and defining new ones. Experiences will also get deeper, connecting more detailed user information and actions with the deepest parts of the enterprise. And the enterprise will respond with an alphabet soup, of CMS - content management systems, DMM - digital marketing management, DAM - digital asset management, and seasoned with ERP, KM, CRM and BI. All with a healthy dose of ROI.

Email Experience

One man's spam is another man's spumoni. So how do you turn pulverized meat in a can into a delightful ice cream treat? Make no doubt about it, spam has wrecked the world of email, but customers still need billing reminders, people still want newsletters, and the Nigerian prince still wants money. A smart user experience professional understands the technical limitations and best practices necessary to leverage email as a marketing and communications tool.

Email is a discipline in and of itself. Many times the copy needs a direct response bent. Companies need to ensure that they are deliverable and not labeled as spam. Complex dynamic link strategies are needed for tracking. Web page counterparts may be necessary if email does not render properly for the user.

142

Experience Optimization

This may be arguably the toughest skill of all. Experience optimization is the ability to look at user data, system performance and research all within the context of the user experience, and then decide how to make it better. Inevitably a brand will get the low-hanging fruit. Usability sessions, email feedback and common sense will knock out the "duh" problems. After all of the easy stuff is done, metrics within any experience will reach a point of stasis (assuming the user base remains constant). The most valuable UX professionals are the ones with the gut intuition of how to tweak the interface, functions, data sources, or offering to move the "stuck" numbers.

Information Architecture

Great, great information architecture ranges from incredible big picture analysis of users and information structures to looking at digital experiences at the near-pixel level. Starting on the big end: Think of all of the different users of a large financial institution's website. One person may want to check their savings balance while another is interested in funding a large expansion of a business. The site may need to answer thousands of questions and support hundreds of user tasks. Now imagine the product line of an industrial supplier, or the inventory of a large retailer. Think about the product numbers, sizes, descriptions, availability, images, documentation, etc., etc. That's a lot of information! How does it fit together? Are there commonalities? What are the differences? Put this in the context of a web page: How can information be arranged on the page? What pieces of information need to be visible and in close proximity? What information can be hidden?

143

Volumes have been written about information architecture, but enough cannot be said about the value that a great information architect brings to a project.

Infrastructure Integration

Infrastructure integration is an understanding of how front-end user experiences interact with back-end infrastructure. This can be as simple as how the inventory on a catalog web site stays up-to-date and as complicated as an interface being completely constructed on the fly from assets in a digital asset management system.

As experiences become more real-time and better integrated with off-line interactions, the necessity for infrastructure integration becomes a more pressing mandate. Think of a person booking a trip through a corporate travel service and then logging on to the airline's web site to check their frequent flyer miles: How long should it take for that account to be credited? A day? A few hours? A few minutes? To a consumer: immediately. Individuals do not sense the boundaries of IT systems, so to them, no lag time should exist. At all.

Don't forget about integration with physical systems such as shipping or even business processes like call center staff training. Many people have experienced the twilight zone of calling an 800 number with a question about the web site only to have the rep say, "Whaaaa??? They changed the website—this is all new to me."

Integrated Business Knowledge

Senior business leadership will look to user experience professionals to help the company make smart bets. Technology

144

is changing so quickly that case studies, best practices and consultant opinions will need to be married to the intuition of user experience professionals who have insight into the business. Ground breaking innovations are difficult to define with traditional CBA techniques. Think iPod. Think Google. Think Flickr. Think YouTube. Could the shape of these really be predicted by looking into the past? A better guess is that the vision of the experience within the market dictated the future for each.

Interaction Design

Digital experiences have long since moved past the point of passive viewing or reading. People now *do* things online and on mobile devices. Interaction design is an understanding of how they do stuff and how to help them do it. This can be as focused as an examination of input devices such as drop downs or fields, and it can be as broad as a looking at how all of the interaction opportunities on a page or screen fit together. It can also get big and look across multiple tasks and screen flows—even across multiple channels throughout the customer life cycle.

Tip: Don't limit the interpretation of "design" to the look and feel. Design here is a more holistic view of the behaviors and parameters of the experience.

Multi-Site, Multi-Experience, Multi-Touch and Partner Management

The pure, public facing term for this is Customer Experience Management. In digital terms this means that users will cross multiple web sites that belong to a company; employees will cross multiple systems; and the digital experiences of partners such as distributors and retailers will become an integral part of the business. Imagine a manufacturer of small gourmet coffee makers. The company may have different web sites for different product lines, use a digital asset management system so the marketing staff and retail channels have access to the latest images, and sell products at brick and mortar retail web sites (like Target.com), at e-tailers (like Amazon.com), on their own sites, and at electronic kiosks in a mall. The variety of digital experiences can be made dimensional with measures of task, frequency, recency and outcome.

Online Media Buying

The contemporary online media buying pro is part statistician, part cultural anthropologist and part user experience guru. Online media is bringing remarkable and diverse opportunities to brands. Behavioral targeting and the ability to hyper-segment down to the keyword level changes the media game that marketers have known for so long. As the opportunities become more complex, so do the strategies, tools, contract negotiations, budgets, test methodologies and performance metrics. On the web, companies initially monitored clickthroughs, then moved to viewthroughs, and now are employing complex portfolio management techniques to monitor traffic productivity.

Pay for Performance Online Advertising

Google has made a fortune with the concept of pay-per-click advertising and provided brands with a scalable, predictable form of advertising. The concept is simple: A person enters a keyword on a search engine and sees a list of results. Giving the regular "free" results a comfy UI hug is a ring of paid advertisements, typically at the top of the page, and down the right column. If a user clicks on one of these

146

paid ads, the advertiser coughs up the dough. The amount is set through a bidding process. If the user does not click, the advertiser gets the free exposure. Sounds simple right? Not really. When done correctly, the brand can squeeze immense benefits out of this form of advertising by using complex bidding strategies, managing a universe of hundreds or thousands of words and phrases, continually optimizing the listings to get good productive clicks (not just high volume clickers) and artfully managing the landing page or entry point to the site.

Cost (Pay) Per Click programs are surrounded by many other types of pay for performance programs including cost per sale, per lead, per conversion, and so on.

Project Management

As user experiences become more integrated with company systems and new technologies raise the bar for user expectations, project managers are faced with new challenges for requirements gathering, scope control, resource management and quality assurance. Projects may reach deeper into company systems. Projects may require team members with radically different talents. Projects may need to very accurately satisfy the needs of wildly divergent user bases. Underpinning all of these concerns are the time-tested issues of sliding delivery dates, change orders and budget controls.

RIA Strategy and Development

Traditional user experience thinking has been built around pages and screens. Web sites had pages and, of course, computer-based experiences had screens. In fact, many of the devices and labels which are nearly engrained into the minds of users, such as "next," "previous" and "home" are the product of these linear or treed structures. The web was also saddled with the challenge of data and interactions making the round trip between the user and the server. Rich Internet Applications, or RIAs, mitigate the lag effect of information moving up and downstream by intelligently mixing the data and interaction at the user (client) level. In other words more of the mojo occurs on the user's machine. As a result, the experience becomes more fluid and dynamic. A.k.a. "rich."

RIAs require a different mindset from the project team for every step from conceptualization through production. The strategist needs to understand what is possible and practical. For example: Would any market risk be involved if the RIA downloaded the prices of all accessories related to a particular product just so the user could play "this-or-that" when deciding what to put into their shopping cart? The interface designer needs to understand how all of the permutations of a rich experience could be displayed within the interface. Content creators will need to understand how to construct and optimize video, sound, animation and special effects for delivery within an RIA. The developers need to understand Flash, AJAX and other rich applications.

Just like the early years of the web, hundreds of poor RIAs will be let loose on unsuspecting users until true best practices and production strategies come to fruition.

Rights

When content of any kind becomes digital, it becomes easy to steal. (Some people call it "sharing.") The infractions range from the innocent to the downright dirty. In the world of music, record labels have struggled to find the correct

148

level of rights management. If the system is too complex, users have a difficult time downloading and enjoying their music. If the parameters are too lenient, files are endlessly swapped with no revenue realized. The possible wrongs of rights go beyond copyright. A competent UX professional needs to understand new systems like the Creative Commons, intellectual property, trademarks, domain squatting and more. Unlike other types of business issues, new case law is being created every day, so the "rules of thumb" are only now being formed.

Search Engine Optimization

No concept is more widely misunderstood than search engine optimization. The goal is simple: Get to #1 on Google and other search engines for relevant, productive terms. How does that happen? This is where it gets messy. In the early days, search engine optimization was just about tweaking your pages in a way that made search engines fall in love with your site. It was a cats and mice game. Sites were relentlessly competing with each other and continually tweaking their pages based upon what the other sites were doing and what was most recently learned about the search engines. These characteristics such as copy tweaking, link-naming and others are now known as "on-page attributes."

Search engines soon began to include other factors in their formulas. The Grand Daddy of them all is Google's page rank which looks at the number and "value" of inbound links. These other attributes are referred to as "off-page attributes" since they are not a part of the site itself. Off-page attributes are not as easy to manipulate, but that does not stop people from trying.

Search engine optimization grows more complex everyday, and as the world gets ever and evermore connected, the stakes get higher. SEO done right can created immense bottom line value. When done wrong, a brand can be damaged, and entire web efforts may need to be scrapped. Blogs, web sites, conventions and numerous books cover the world of SEO. (Go to an SEO conference and linger in the bathroom. Creepy, yes, but you'll hear some enlightening things.) You can't learn it in a week. Hire a pro, but choose very carefully.

Team Leadership

"Hey, you designers, I want your designs to be 52% more attractive." "You writers, get 10% more on-brand and throw in 5% more freshness." "Let's get more innovative, but let me see the business case first." "Oh, developers, don't spend any time learning about the emerging technologies that won't work, only pick out the ones that are destined to be forces in the market." "And by the way, all you creative types, don't act THAT way." Obviously, these approaches will never work.

Running a user experience team requires a different set of people skills, technical knowledge and performance management strategy. The good leader understands how deep their technical or discipline knowledge should be, how to communicate the vision rather than specify tactics, how to feed the team's passion for learning with the reality of making the rubber hit the road every day, how to nurture a productive and innovative environment, and how to assess, critique and improve work quality.

150

Thought Leadership

The world of user experience changes constantly. Cool to-day is stool tomorrow. (Ya know, crappy.) Thought leadership is about understanding applicability and longevity as much as it is about being informed on what is new. People with hunger, inquisitiveness and a demonstrated, ongoing insight into emerging trends and technologies are rare birds indeed.

UI (User Interface) Design and Art Direction

Cool, Usability and *Brand* walk into a bar. The bartender says, "What are you guys?" The group says, "We're a web site." The bartender smirks, "Liars. I've never seen you guys all together before."

This is the challenge of user interface design and art direction: making a digital experience cool, usable and brand-appropriate. This extends far beyond visual compliance to include behavioral consistency. The scope also goes far beyond a single experience, such as a site. Today's UX design team must look across multiple touch points, sites and channels.

Being a great, experienced graphic designer is not enough. An interface designer needs to have the ability to create a brand-appropriate look and feel for a page/screen with the appropriate recognition of usability, information architecture and interaction.

Usability

Usability is a complex discipline that weaves through the conceptualization and development of experiences through final testing and future optimization. It includes the exami-

151

nation of all aspects of an experience intended to help the user achieve easy, accurate and complete outcomes. Usability can focus on the smallest details of an interface like button labels, and can also include more complicated endeavors such as running detailed usability sessions designed to objectively test experiences. Sometimes usability requires deep expertise mixed with gut intuitions and other times it requires rigorous testing methodologies and bullet-proof data analysis.

Usability issues are often a company's most overlooked quick-wins. A seasoned professional can typically look at a user experience and immediately find usability improvements that business people, IT professionals and other groups miss.

User-Centered Analysis

User experience data can be very difficult to understand. For example, two different users each look at the home page of a web site and leave after ten seconds. One found the phone number they were looking for while the other did not quite understand the labels used on the product categories. Neither one *did* anything, but the first had a positive brand experience, and the other had a negative brand experience. According to the data, however, they look exactly the same. Analytics is tricky because the interpretation of the information needs to be sound from a statistical point of view, but the intent and structure of the experience needs to be included as well.

A strong analytics person will understand the current state of the experience, how it has changed, and the market while

Kenneth J. Weiss

being highly competent with the methodologies of data collection and the tools needed for analysis.

User Experience Strategy

User experience is not just thinking about what can be coded, or what can be "messaged" or what can be collected, or what people can be made to do. User experience strategy is the ability to conceptualize digital experiences where the goals of the user can be accomplished while creating business value from the interaction. If a person wants to be really good at user experience strategy, knowledge of everything in this book and more is essential. Tall order? Yes.

Web Analytics

Web analytics is the collection and interpretation of web site data. The first step is to make sure the web site or application produces data that can be recorded. As interactions become richer and more of the functionality is powered from within the browser, detailed data is not always reported back to the server, the typical collection point. Even advanced, page-based tracking is not able to pick up the all of the nuances of richer interactions. Provided the data is collected, the next step is to eliminate the garbage. Competitors' use of the system, internal network traffic, monitoring activity and more needs to be purged. Even when the data is clean, some degree of interpretation is needed. If one user needed an email address and the other was bored by the web site and simply left, both sessions may seem identical in the data. In reality, one was successful and the other was not. The craft of web analytics requires the ability to credibly work with statistics while objectively interpreting the user experience.

Web Development

The web has come a long way since HTML 1.0. In the beginning, the web had the presentation abilities of an early word processor: lots of flush left presentation, bold and italics. The web was also rife with itty-bitty pictures that were perfect for shoving down phone lines. Now, the web is a complex montage of images, video, audio, interaction, messaging and functionality. Entry level designers used to be defined by their ability to competently drive WYSIWYG (What You See Is What You Get) web page editors. Fast forward to contemporary times and the bar is set a little higher each day. Programming techniques have successfully loosed the content from the code providing new opportunities for quick, standards-compliant development. CSS, Actionscript, XML and other types of coding are basic competencies for web developers, and a good developer understands how the web page or app can create an ideal user experience.

To be good, companies and individuals need to stay on top of their game through continual training, working with other skilled developers, reading blogs, dissecting other pages. To be good and stay good—nothing takes the place of building lots and lots of pages and sites.

You, SME and Me

Subject Matter Experts (SMEs), the people who really understand a particular product, process, IT system, application or market segment, will be essential team members on every digital experience project in the future. Building an online customer service function? Getting it 90% right is no longer acceptable in the customers' eyes. Users will want to tap in to the knowledge of a seasoned rep. Trying to build

154

an online product comparison function? Product and sales pros will need to be integrated into the earliest discussions about the creation of the experience. UX pros will need to understand how to engage these resources as integral parts of projects.

Understanding the Quality of Any User Experience - the Big Picture

An evaluation of any digital experience needs to start with the basics. Wow, that sounds incredibly simple. But, wow, it is incredibly difficult. The tendency is to jump to the tactical level: the colors, the fonts, the pictures. The key is to begin by taking a breath and reviewing the experience's most elemental aspects.

User-Centered Design

Any successful user experience must be centered on the user. Again, sounds simple enough, but user needs can easily be overshadowed by corporate perspectives, stakeholder predispositions and team member personalities.

Ask the challenging questions: Would the interface make sense to the user? Are the terms being used "our terminology" or "their terminology"? Is the information complete, accurate and truthful? Have the users requested the content and functionality that is being offered? Conversely, have they requested something that is not being offered? Were any shortcuts used to make production easier but will make the user work harder?

Analyze every aspect from the user's perspective. Do not just think of a single user, think of every type of user in the

155

original scope of the project. Can they execute the tasks? Do they have the right amount of technical knowledge? Are they equipped with the right computer, cell phone or portable device? Some experiences must be "walk up and use." That means the user should be able to effectively use the experience with no training, background or knowledge.

Truly appreciating user-centered design may be incredibly difficult for a person who knows the industry, business, product or customer well. Objectivity can be difficult to kindle and keep.

Usability testing is essential. In a perfect world, paper prototypes, functional iterations and final versions are all tested with the proper users. Usability testing is an investment, but it should be valued as highly as IT infrastructure, professional interface design and content development.

Equivalent Anonymity

Users believe they are entitled to a certain amount of anonymity when interacting with digital experiences, especially on the web. Identity is a form of capital. If a system requires a user to divulge information, the user will expect something of value in exchange. Even if a company has the best intentions, the user will be skeptical. This is not about, "will the company bug me in the future?" or some form of "big brother" fear. It is simply business. In a world of over six billion people, information about a particular individual is worth something.

When reviewing an experience be aware of any place where the scale of what is a fair exchange (from the user's perspective) tips in the wrong direction. This might be as simple as

156

requiring a registration on a web site to download a technical paper. That would be fair or wouldn't it?

Organization and Navigation

Where should content and functions be placed in the overall experience? How are pieces of content related? What relationships do the users see? How should the navigation be structured? What labels should be used? What navigation devices should be incorporated in the interface? Drop downs? Fly out menus? An experimental interface? These ideas are part of a misunderstood and underappreciated discipline called Information Architecture.

When done correctly, the product of great information architecture is nearly imperceptible. Content relationships will feel effortless. Users will quickly be able to find related, relevant pieces of information, and information that holds multiple relationships will always feel accessible but not redundant. The navigation will feel like an extension of the users' thoughts and finger tips. Moving from one section of the experience to the next will be simple. Returning to a point in the experience after a delightful tangent will require no test of the memory or imagination.

Information architecture also extends to the multi-step tasks known as flows. Well-constructed flows should be intuitive and effortless. The interactions will be in the logical order, with not too few or too many steps – and the outcomes will be predictable and accurate. Errors should be understood easily, and the user should be able to recover easily.

157

Expected Locations and Mental Models

Quick! Where is the home link on any web page? Upper left? How did you know? Well, that's where it always is, right? Yes and no. Back in '95 it might have been anywhere, but slowly users came to expect it in certain places and more web developers started to put it there. Similar expectations have developed around header, footer and secondary navigation, search fields, log-in fields and checkout buttons. Don't outguess the users. Don't let creativity and originality pound the proverbial snot out of usability. Content and functions should be in the expected places. (From the users' perspective, remember?)

Good user experience strategy can also capitalize on the mental models shared by users. In the early days of the web, interfaces were straight metaphorical interpretations of physical places and objects: the lobby of a building, the drawers within a desk, etc. Today's users can apply more complex models of how things work to digital experiences allowing mental models to be more dimensional. For instance a mental model of a restaurant kitchen would include raw materials (ingredients) management, labor, equipment, energy and finished meals forming complete economic transactions. A digital experience using this model could draw upon the order of events, likely outcomes, types of participants, etc.

Defined Outcomes

What is supposed to happen when the user interacts with the system? The outcomes should be defined from user, business and technical standpoints. Sure, there will always be instances when exploration, innovation and experimentation necessitate that an experience will have no defined out-

158

come – and this may be where true breakthroughs happen – but for the most part, outcomes should be rigorously defined. If success and failures are not defined, the experience will be doomed to the realm of subjective opinion.

Brand Language

A brand is more than just a recipe of fonts, colors and pictures. The look and feel of the experience, the way it presents itself and behaves, should embody the brand. It is possible for a user experience to have the right "look" but not be on brand. It is also possible that the experience delivers great content, functionality and value to the user, but is not visually on brand.

Check the colors and fonts, certainly. But also look at the imagery, tonality, consistency, accuracy and overall quality. Think of the experience as an employee, location, package, video, phone script or an impassioned speech from the company owner. Is it on brand?

Wow-Factor or Super Practical

Every company wants their web site or other interactive experience to be "wow." Is "wow" glitzy, exciting, beautiful and senses-engaging? Or is it just really, really easy, quick and useful? A company might say one set of adjectives is a wow, and the customers another. Sometimes super-practical is the wow everyone should want. Think about checking the balance in your savings account, making a stock trade or changing your health benefits. What should "wow" feel like for those?

UX Quality - Looking a Little Closer

Once the big picture has been reviewed, smaller concepts contained within the pages or screens can be examined.

Affordance

This one is quick but tricky: If a user can interact with an element on the page, the element should indicate that by the way it looks.

Take, for example, a few words of text. Maybe you can click on that, maybe you can't. Make it blue and add an underline – everyone knows it's a link. The color and underline are the affordance.

Consider a simple drop down box, the downward-pointing arrow provides the affordance.

Try deconstructing one: A big rectangular graphic with text, a shiny texture, smoothed edges and a drop shadow that raises it off the page - that's probably a button. What happens if you take away:

The text?

The shiny texture?

The smoothed edges?

The drop shadow?

At some point it is no longer a button to the user, because you are taking away the affordance.

Affordance is getting trickier by the minute. So many new techniques for interaction are possible. In fact, the most valued experiences may be constructed of interaction devices that the user has never seen. *But*, they should know that they *can* interact because each device should have some level of affordance.

Stand up. Walk around the desk. Take a fresh look at the interface. Would, should, could the user know that they can interact with an element on the page?

Yes? It has affordance.

No? Then you have a little problem.

Chunking and Grouping

Items, functions and content that hold relationships should be placed together within an interface. This is called chunking.

Chunking benefits the user in a number of ways. First, it provides a way for users to quickly sort the information on a page. Rather than seeing twenty, thirty or forty elements on a page, users can more easily grasp a page that is comprised of a smaller number of sets, a.k.a. chunks.

Chunking also gives users an immediate shortcut to related elements. For instance, if a user was looking for a particular SUV on a manufacturer's web site, finding a similar SUV within the interface probably means the sought after one is close by.

Chunking provides users with a nice way to arrange items in their memory as they use the system. Where was an element? Check the chunk.

Chunking creates great predictability. Where should something be? Check the chunk that held similar items.

The term "grouping" is sometimes used interchangeably with chunking. Other practiced user experience pros might think of multiple chunks belonging to a group. A sound concept—use it if you'd like.

Chunks can be created with rule lines, the use of white space, fields of color, common type treatments, etc. Once a chunking convention is used on a page, it should be used consistently throughout the system. Be careful how much is placed in a chunk. Research shows that chunks fail to provide any benefits to the user when crammed with more than seven items.

White Space

White space can be used to separate chunks, provide breathing room around elements, and serve as an invisible structure for the page. Think of the white spaces surrounding a column of text. Nothing is really there, but the white space serves as a border and lends structure. White space, when placed in staggered increments, suggests the subordinate relationships of a line of text, paragraph, list or picture.

When used correctly white space not only provides functional benefits, it also can allow the interface to feel simple, relaxing and "clean."

White space is not always white. Any color used to an appreciable degree within an interface can serve as the white space.

Conspicuity/Visibility

Every element within an interface competes for the attention of the user. Even in well-balanced interfaces, tertiary elements including borders, soft colors, footers and disclaimers require visual processing. Any element can be judged by how conspicuous or visible it is on the page. Simply stated, will the user notice it? This is critical for functional elements such as buttons and links.

What harms the visibility of key elements? Lack of white space, competing colors, competing shapes, poor placement on the screen (especially below the scroll), lack of contrast in typography, no range in hierarchy, excessive animations and too much texture.

Remember that visibility is not necessarily a function of size. Imagine a tiny fly on a sheet of clean paper. Pretty visible, huh?

Poor visibility could be a telltale sign that the interface was designed by a person with traditional design skills rather than interactive design skills who favored visual harmony and style over usability, or it could be the result of a stakeholder who thought that more choices would lead to more activity.

State Awareness

Experiences are becoming more interactive, more dimensional and less linear.

163

Imagine a person using a "build you own vehicle" function on an automotive web site. Interrupted by a knock at the door, they return a few minutes later, and ask the question, "Where was I?" The experience, the web site in this case, needs to communicate its state.

State awareness is different than navigation orientation. Showing someone where they are in the navigation is rooted in physical boundaries - how far a user is from the home page, which section they are in, etc. State awareness needs to accommodate experiences that are varied and fluid during a single session and over multiple uses. Imagine an online role-playing game where the other characters and the environment are constantly changing. How does a user return to the game and understand how things may have changed while at the same time enjoying the challenge of catching up?

Mode Awareness

Some types of digital experiences can change modes, behaving in a different way in each mode. Inputs can be different, the display of information different, etc. The easiest example is the old multi-function calculator. It worked great if you knew what you were doing. Accidentally switch it to the rocket-science-guy mode, and it was impossible to add two numbers together. Sometimes public kiosks are inadvertently switched from user mode to administrator mode. When happenstance drags the next user along, they are faced with a log-in screen. Other modes are more subtle - an intranet application might exist in manager, team lead and team member modes, with each mode offering slightly different flavors of tasks.

Changing modes can be great for experienced users, allowing them to rapidly flip to "expert" mode. Mode changing can be effectively applied to special devices, such as purpose-built hand-held computers, but should typically NOT be a feature of the average web site, CD-ROM or walk-up-and-use computer application.

Examining the Details

Navigation Execution

Good information architecture is a product of big picture thinking as well as a vigilant eye on the execution of the navigation. This does not mean that only one correct solution for navigation schemes exists.

A common arrangement for navigation is a hierarchical approach with nav elements across the top (global nav) and links stacked along the side of the interface (secondary) dividing the site into categories and subcategories.

Processes, tours, photo galleries and other content may be arranged in a linear format with back, forward, and auto-play controls.

Other content may be arranged along two-dimensional matrices, such as the details of a company's operating units being organized by both type and geographic location.

Rich media technologies can be used to organize information along multiple dimensions.

Smaller sites may be fully meshed together with all pages linking to each other.

Some experimental, entertainment and game sites may use abstract or story-based navigation structures.

Some common navigation elements include:

"You Are Here" Indicators - These can be small graphics such as arrows, changes in typography and other similar conventions to let the user know "You are here." A well conceived experience knows that a person may not always enter via the home page or main menu. Imagine that user who drops in at a lower level: the "you are here" indicator shows them where they are, and the rest of the nav elements should give a sense of their overall place within the structure.

Waypoints - These are visual elements that act as landmarks within a site. For example, the graphic page headers on category pages within a large catalog web site will look different from the home page and product pages, and each will have a slightly different look.

Breadcrumbs - Breadcrumbs are the small sequential lines of navigation that are placed near the top of the page, usually separated by arrows or carets. They > look > like > this . When breadcrumbs were first used many years ago, they typically were created dynamically and showed the user their path of travel through the site. Since navigation patterns differed, the breadcrumbs were different for each user. Today, breadcrumbs tend to show the hierarchal relationship of pages and functions within an experience.

Control Selectivity

Users should be able to interact with controls such as drop downs, links, buttons and more without accidentally acti-

166

vating (selecting) other controls. A common problem is proximity: they are just too dang close together. This is yet another area where restraint is needed. More choices might seem like a good idea, but lack of control selectivity makes a crammed interface more frustrating for the user.

Control Sensitivity

Many controls have simple inactive or active states. An example would be a button. You have either clicked on it or you haven't.

Other devices such as sliders may need to be placed at very precise points on the path in order to create the specific, desired outcome.

Typography

Typography is the selection, treatment and use of fonts within a user interface, along with the overall arrangement of text elements. On the web, typography was previously limited by the number of fonts that systems could display. Designers and developers could specify a font but a variety of limitations put its final appearance in question. The only way to create some degree of certainty was to execute the text as graphics, but this had limitations for users with disabilities and the practice was a hindrance to good search engine optimization. Fortunately browsers and operating systems are becoming more adept at displaying varying typefaces, and other types of digital experiences are less subject to the limitations of the web.

Good typography also has a role in usability. The font, size, as well as treatments such as italics, alignment (how it is placed in relation to other elements), orientation (vertical or horizontal) and a variety of other factors contribute to the legibility and usability of the interface.

Often when an interface seems to lack a certain level of polish or expressiveness, typography is the culprit. Typical mistakes include too many fonts and the over-manipulation of fonts in a way that obscures the message or damages the usability of the system.

When it comes to typography, think restraint, think brand standards. Think usability.

Foreshadowing, Consistency and Predictability

When an experience is constructed correctly the user can learn as they go. The learning cues can be almost imperceptible, but highly effective.

Foreshadowing is the strategic use of colors, location, behavior and interactions designed to show the user what is coming next, and what might be expected from them on the coming pages or screens. Often, it is this understanding of what is about to happen that keeps the user comfortable, on track and committed.

Consistency puts users at ease, forestalls any guesswork, and lets users focus on the task. Consistency applies to all parts of the experience: where things are located, how data is shown, how they should interact with controls, etc. If it sounds boring, it is not. A user is more pleased with a successful outcome than a never-ending series of curve balls designed to "surprise" them and make the experience "interesting."

Predictability sounds dull too. But it is not. Imagine a user whose checking account balance was displayed a little differently each time they used their online banking web site. "WTF?" They would say. (You know, "What's that format?") Seriously, the constant changes to interfaces, outcomes or processes erode confidence and brand affinity.

Images

Brands have always had the opportunity to create original photography. Some of it was very expensive. The economies of digital photography have greatly expanded the amount of photography available in the marketplace. Not all of it is great, or even good.

Typical trouble spots with images:

Different photography styles throughout an experience.

Using stock photography that turns up on competitors' experiences.

Failing to keep up with rights issues.

Cultural issues popping up in shots. (What side of the road are those people driving on?)

Employees appearing in images and then leaving the company.

A discontinued product appearing in a group shot.

Interfaces all suffer when images are used to create tonality and mood, but are confusing to users who try to interpret them as subject matter.

Grammar and Typos

These are bad. It takes a really good proofreader to catch them all. (Okay, how many did you find in that sentence?)

When Things Go Wrong

Good planning can allow for things to go wrong and soften the blow to the brand. After all, even the best constructed and managed workflows miss a problem or two. Hopefully both frequency and severity are low.

Graceful Degradation

Sometimes web pages, kiosks, desktop widgets and other digital experiences do not quite work correctly. How badly they are broken becomes the real question. Planning for graceful degradation means assuming what might break within a system, and determining how the system will react (hopefully). For example, if a web site uses Flash, but the user's browser does not have the right version, will the site still be usable? Is the user made aware that something is not quite right? Will they be able to adjust their understanding of the experience so they can complete their task, or are they simply left puzzled?

Missing images, code that operates differently from browser to browser, video that may or may not play, user-contributed content that can be unexpectedly removed, backend systems that go down, and a variety of other factors make graceful degradation a must.

Undo

If a user makes a mistake, they may want to simply undo what they've just done. Simple enough. But…they must realize that they have done something incorrectly, and the functionality that provides the undo function must be very easy to understand and use. Sometimes the instruction line is a question: "Are you sure you want to...." Other times it is a statement: "By clicking this you will..."

Even if the user understands the options, the system must be easy to use. Should the "yes" button be above below or beside the cancel button? How close together are the buttons? A few pixels?

Undo is not always forever. Sometimes a redo is necessary. "Oops! I *did* want to keep that in the shopping cart." Processes with multiple sequential steps may need a multiple undo. An undo also may need to be selective, allowing the user to undo only a portion of the experience.

Explicit Destruction

On occasion a user really wants to completely undo something or totally discard their progress on a long sequence of tasks. They want explicit destruction. This is a clear, obvious series of interactions where the system and the user know that this is "buh-bye" forever. The site or the system will present one or more chances to turn back, e.g., "By clicking this button you will delete all of the changes you've made to your online health care coverage account – do you wish to delete these changes?" Followed by, "Your changes have been deleted. Click here to return to the main menu to start again."

Explicit destruction is useful when the user absolutely needs to know that all of their activities are being eliminated.

171

A Few Nice Touches

Autofill/Auto Complete

A nice touch in forms and systems is to make the experience remember or automatically provide pertinent content. Most people have experienced a very simple version of this when completing a web form: the web site pre-fills a zip code or area code based upon an earlier user action or piece of stored data.

This practice can get much more advanced through the inclusion of complex stored data or by accessing data from external systems.

For instance, a system might access the value of a home, credit report and the names of people living in a household when a user applies for a car loan online. This is intended to make the experience less laborious for the user while providing complete and more consistent data for the lender.

Convenience must be balanced against the "big brother creepy factor." The experience must also be carefully constructed to make sure that the user verifies the accuracy of any data that is pre-filled.

Controlled Vocabulary

Words, even in the digital age, remain incredibly important. Although beautiful in their diversity, a simple system of carefully chosen and consistently used words and phrases is helpful in user experiences.

A controlled vocabulary is not always popular with traditional marketers. "It seems redundant." "It's off-brand!" "It has no personality." Yes, yes, yes, but a happy outcome is always better than a confused user.

Economy of Effort

Economy of effort has two parts: Within the walls of the organization it means that the effort and expense involved in creating the system should be commensurate with the value it creates for users and the business advantage it creates for the brand within the marketplace. If it is wrong, it is busy work and folly. Secondly, when viewed from the perspective of the user, it means the system should only take the correct, typically low, amount of effort to use. Too much, and the user is dejected. Too little valued, and whoa...brand damage.

Economy of Expression

Differences in the interface should be meaningful and apparent. If one button is blue and the other is green, that should mean something. The expression, the countenance of the interface, should use small differences very effectively to communicate. This economy of expression will make the system easier to use. The user will spend less time attempting to distill the interface and filtering information from changes that are changes simply for the sake of visual variety. Like cooking, an overabundance of spices does not provide flavor, it only makes the user say "yuck."

Getting Adaptive

Adaptivity is something that users commonly see on desktop computers. The operating system shows what files a person has opened recently and Word lists the most recently used fonts at the top of the fonts drop down list. In both

Slightware - The Next Great Threat to Brands

instances the experience is demonstrating its ability to adapt to the user.

Adaptivity can help the experience as long as the changes, and more importantly, the reasons for the changes are evident to the user.

When adaptive behavior is engineered into experiences correctly, users can more quickly select and execute tasks. Users can also more effectively use the system over time.

The Case for Future Proofing Your Brand

This is the point where "Slightware Stopping The Next Great Threat to Brands" might look silly. Why? Because any predictions about the future of technology may look silly at some point.

"I think there is a world market for maybe five computers."
Thomas Watson, chairman of IBM, 1949

"Computers in the future may weigh no more than 1.5 tons."
Popular Mechanics, 1949

"There is no reason in the world anyone would want a computer in their home. No reason."
Ken Olsen, Chairman, DEC, 1977

Brand predictions can be silly, too.

"Let's revise the formula for Coke and call it New Coke."
Fired branding-guy, circa 1985

Instead of falling in line with these missives, this tome will try the Alan Kay approach: "The best way to predict the future is to invent it."

Almost every user experience over time will feel less relevant and become dated. For brands, that dated feeling can be a very damaging feeling.

A good - really good, website might have a shelf life of a year. (That's a could-be-silly prediction right there.) Other experiences such as applications, games, kiosks and mobile experience will inevitably fall victim to changes in technology, user preference, execution style or all of the above. Maybe a year. Maybe more. Maybe less. Brands will need to continually reinvest in their digital expressions, and harness the ever-emerging possibilities.

Tools for Future Proofing

Many of the people who read the following paragraphs will say, "Wow, that is amazing!" The really amazing part? Many people who read the following paragraphs will say, "I've been working on that technology for <u>years!</u> Wait until you see what is <u>really</u> in the future!"

Intelligent Assumptions

The concept of personalization is nearly as old as the modern interface. Users have been able to pick content, choose colors, arrange panels and incorporate tools and widgets. Experiences have also been programmed with behavioral technology to "guess" what users might want to do. Content

175

and advertising technologies also take huge amounts of aggregated data and the past actions of users to personalize the experience. Do these approaches work? For some people, in some situations they work splendidly. Other times? Well, yeah, no.

The coming generations of personalization technology will have deeper, more situational memory, make smarter conditional assumptions and recognize users' personal modality. For example, the next generation corporate intranet will understand the difference between "I'm killing time checking email before a meeting" versus "I need to look up a healthcare provider because my ill wife is on the phone." These intelligent assumptions will be shared across all types of devices from computers to mobile phones to appliances. If your applications at the office recognize that you are having a bad day at work you may come home to a blender that is already happily buzzing away making a margarita.

3D Interfaces

Visually implied 3D elements are an essential part of today's interface design arsenal. When a user sees tabs in an interface, they don't really believe that there are multiple layers of stuff stacked on the screen, but they understand the intent. The little ridges on scroll bars really don't rise above the rest of the graphic, but they look like they do.

In the future interfaces will be truly three-dimensional. This will start as 3D objects on a flat screen which can be manipulated dimensionally and will evolve to holographic-like projections which float in space before the user. No giggling please. Researchers are already experimenting with this technology.

Touch and Multi-Touch Interfaces

Touch screen interfaces are nothing new. Bank machines and self-service kiosks at grocery stores and airports have made touch screens commonplace. The next step is multi-touch interfaces which allow multiple users to provide input at one time. This technology keeps track of a steady stream of inputs from multiple users even as they perform difficult and interconnected tasks. Imagine a team of military doctors performing surgery remotely on a badly wounded patient using a multi-touch interface connected to an array of robotic surgical devices thousands of miles away! How about a gaggle of kids playing a game at a children's party center? Both will be really cool.

Kinetic Sensibility

Kinetic properties are already appearing on interfaces and give interface objects physical, motion-oriented behaviors that people understand from every day life. For instance, a person nudging an icon on a kinetic interface might expect it to move, drift and then come to a gradual stop. This is the same behavior that exists in the physical world. Kinetics are powerful because they capitalize on a vast universal language of how things work that transcends languages and cultures. Increasingly improved kinetics will allow elements to be pushed, stacked, pinned, shuffled, oriented, etc. What an amazing collection of meaning!

Dynamic Synthetic Realities

Multi-player games such as "World of Warcraft" and "Second Life" have been offering users a chance to step into new virtual realities and "play." You can kill characters, have relationships (or at least "relations"), conduct commerce and even build brands. This concept of realities will continually

177

evolve within interfaces. Think of the interfaces used to manage complex stock portfolios: the tools are there—the data is there. In the not-too-distant future, the experience will include a staff of synthetic helpers. Rather than simply clicking your way through a series of screens, a digital minion will perform the work for you. "Mr. Elasticity, calculate my downside risk of moving assets from international tech funds to European financial interests." The resulting data will not be a simple series of charts and numbers, but will include on-demand conversations with synthetic subject matter experts, a bird's eye views of supply chains, interactive models of country economies, and more. Users will be able to prod, poke and test the experience the same way a toddler splashes in the bathtub to see what happens.

Dynamic Tonality

Every good brand has a documented brand voice, and consistency of the brand voice is essential to maintaining the brand. At least that's what common brand logic dictates. In reality, the voice of the brand is tweaked on a daily basis: a salesman for the brand knows the type of delivery that works with a particular customer, a phone rep goes "off script" in an attempt to pacify an irate customer, a public relations pro crafts a press release with a slightly different twist in order to capture the attention of a senior editor. These alterations to the brand voice do happen. In the future, interfaces will do this in a much more controlled and deliberate way in response to the feedback and interactions of a particular user or group of users. This might be a tough genie to stuff back in the bottle when it happens, but it will happen eventually.

Kenneth J. Weiss

New Types of Input

Gesture Based – Soon, all types of gestures will be used to control interfaces. Wink. Nod. Smile. Point. Frown. Shrug. Middle finger. Gesture based input systems will be tailored to people with all types of abilities and disabilities. In the most challenging situations, eye movements, body language and even puffs of breath will be harnessed to allow the user to interact with the user experience.

Voice Control - Voice recognition systems will continue to improve. Structured vocabularies of words and phrases will give way to more fluid, casual language.

A related technology, natural language search (the technical term for search queries comprised of typical questions such as "What is the capital of Sudan?") will merge with voice recognition. Questions of all types will be spoken to control search engines, applications, quiz games and the most basic user experiences.

These new systems will understand moods, sense urgency and differentiate the meanings of the intonations of different people at different times.

Mind/Thought Control - Sounds futuristic and a little creepy, huh? Guess what? It's already here. New types of game controllers allow users to control games through a combination of neural inputs and head gestures. Imagine this coupled with a 3D interface or synthetic reality! Layer on wide area wireless networks, mult-iplayer aspects, and all types of new interfaces. Whoa, what do you "think" about the new product from company XYZ?

179

Aggregated Input - In the old day of television, when black and white game shows were popular fare, outcomes were sometimes decided by the applause meter. Contestants would face off in a challenge and the audience would "vote" by clapping. The loudest applause appointed the winner. This strange social force appeared again in the earliest days of Web 2.0. People gave thumbs up or down, decided who was hot or not, and stories rose and fell on lists based upon votes. These systems of collecting and aggregating input will become more dynamic with instantaneous results. Groups of users will be polled to control the experience.

Sensory and Tactile Feedback

All of these new types of inputs will be accompanied by remarkable feedback. Most people are familiar with "click" sound effects triggered by screen interactions and video game controllers that vibrate in response to game play. Future feedback will respond to users by offering tactical feedback that helps the user perceive nuances in effort and resistance. Other senses will be engaged with smells, temperature changes and a variety of other sensations that connect the users' actions with the interface. Some will be positive. Others will connote problems. The orchestration of all of this feedback will elicit a complete spectrum of feelings and emotions. This will get freaky. Some feedback will even be provided by electrical pulses that interact directly with a user's nervous system.

So What's Stopping Us?

At this point in the book, brand pros, UX aficionados, IT geeks and MBA propeller heads are probably saying "Seems simple enough. Complicated. But, simple enough." If this is true why do so many horrific user experiences still exist?

Ducks

Baby ducks. Really. "Baby Duck Syndrome" is the phrase used to refer to the fact that people tend to stick with interfaces that they first learn. They are like baby ducks just following along. A new version of a software package comes out with dozens of new features and improvements, and what do people say? "I can't find anything." Followed by, "Can I just use the old version?" Now imagine putting a completely different interface on the front end of a fantasy football league. People will hate it! Some for only a while. Some forever.

(Just be careful if you wear a "Kill baby ducks" t-shirt in public.)

Experience Monitoring and Analytics

These new types of interfaces and input devices will create massive amounts of data. The idea of "clicks" will be an understatement of epic proportions. The systems recording the activity will need to be nearly as powerful as those delivering it. The data storage requirements will be massive. Then will come the challenge of cataloging data, dissecting it and analyzing the information. No simple patterns will exist. Commonalities will be hard to identify. Optimizing the experience, the end-goal of any analytics process, will be difficult.

Availability of User Experience Pros

Good UX people are really hard to find. The number of UX rising stars coming out of the nation's best universities capable of leading the charge for these new types of interfaces are rare and command big, big dollars. UX pros already working in the field will need to integrate constant learning and experimentation into their daily habits. Companies operating outside of east coast and west coast hot spots will need to determine how to compete for talent, and more importantly figure out how to keep that talent compensated correctly, challenged and respected.

The network of people around these pros will need to change as well. Writers will need to understand how their work can be enhanced and changed by these systems. Corporate attorneys will need to decide whether dynamic comments uttered by a 3D avatar could be seen by the courts as legally binding promises. Marketers who are used to having rock solid control over the voice of the brand will need to decide how they feel about community voices discussing a brand. Every corner of the organization will need to decide what these new interfaces mean to them.

Usability Planning and Testing

Today's body of usability thinking is rooted in years of studying how people use computers and includes gaming, immersive environments, mobile devices, consumer electronics and even printed documentation. This is a great start, but in order for new interfaces to take hold and produce successful results for both users and brands, usability planning and testing will need to evolve—and quickly. Early working documents such as paper prototypes will need to accurately portray motion, sound and feedback. Observation labs which typically have the subjects seated at a desk will need to allow for users to be more active. The mechanisms for capturing all types of feedback will need to

182

be more robust. Imagine a camera recording the facial expression of a person using the next generation interface of an auto maker's web site. How will joy, amazement and satisfaction be quantified?

Security

Hackers are bad guys. Bad guys doing bad things, but being remarkably interesting as they do them. Some of the tricks are scary and simple. A hacker can go to a company's "Contact Us" web page, grab the code, and send a string of programming commands rather than the form data like name, email address, etc., and presto: the site returns a list of email addresses of everyone who has ever submitted the form. This will not work on every site, but it has worked. When companies plug a hole like this, the hackers move on to the next site, or they enhance their tactics.

The interfaces of the future will create incredibly complex scenarios that could be used to breach a company's IT environment. If an interface will allow users to behave in an almost infinite number of different patterns or sequences, how will the security gurus be able to predict how these actions might be used nefariously? Will IT be in favor of these new interfaces? Will they take a very cautious approach? Will they request that specific capabilities be removed from an interface because of the uncertainties? Guess.

These new interfaces will be wonderful, but even the smallest security breaches can have a massively bad impact on brands. Imagine *one* national talk show host mentioning that someone hacked their account and placed a number of highly controversial titles on their 3D virtual wish list at a major book web site. The host would be very concerned

183

about damage to his or her reputation as a brand, and the publicity would be very damaging to the book site's brand.

User Training

A perfect user experience is perfectly intuitive. That is to say, it requires no training. How many user experiences are perfect? Not many. As interfaces become wonderfully capable and complex, users will need to be able to rapidly understand and effectively use these new innovations. How can you train a person on an interface that is dynamically personalized, affected by other users, shaped by external stimuli and ever-evolving? Good question. Unless the industry wants people to slide back to comfortable, familiar, older technologies the question will need to be answered.

Maintenance and Updating

Many companies can't keep the product copy on their web sites up to date. How about maintaining an entire virtual 3D world or synthetic character?

Often the creation of digital experiences starts with rousing interest from a variety of stakeholders. Good projects keep the momentum going throughout the project. Really great projects are built with a lasting commitment from the organization. An old saying (of my own) goes, "'Website isn't a noun, it's a verb.'"

Underestimating Kids

Kids are great at using new interfaces. They have no preconceived notions. No fear. No hesitancy about jumping in. Doesn't sound like they are being underestimated, right? What people fail to realize is how fast they can ascend in the

Kenneth J. Weiss

worlds of technology and business, and how fast their likes and dislikes become cultural forces.

In Closing

Slightware is big, indeed. Complicated with fuzzy edges. People in every part of an organization who learn about slightware will inevitably say, "That touches my job." Specialists in the areas of marketing, branding and technology probably found some topics in this book far underdeveloped. Some other ideas may have felt very distant and difficult to understand. In some instances, examples were provided to show rock solid learnings while other stories were left open-ended. Slightware is big. The causes are evolving. The solutions are evolving. And the end of this book is just the beginning.

2981564

Made in the USA